JESUS IS ALIVE!

This book is dedicated to my wife, Joanne, who really is co-author of this book, and as well to the members of St. Martin's without whose love and support this venture in faith would not have been possible.

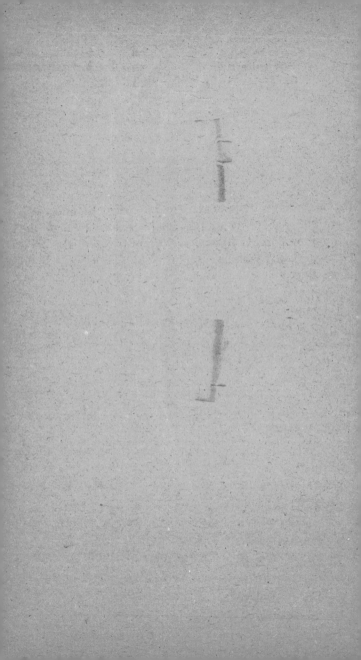

ACKNOWLEDGMENTS

I want to thank everyone who assisted me in preparing this book and especially to:

The congregation and friends of St. Martin's who supported Joanne and me with their prayers and fasting throughout this project;

Grandma Florence who so willingly moved in with our three sons for a week so Joanne could go away with me to write;

Pearl Baker, Helen DeIvernois, and Ruth Mary Eaton for the initial typing; Stanley Higgins for editing; Peg Sandford for final typing of the manuscript;

And all those who so kindly submitted designs for the cover (special thanks to Alan Sandford whose cover was chosen by our publisher).

The Biblical references, unless otherwise stated, are taken by permission of the American Bible Society from *Good News for Modern Man, Today's English Version,* copyrighted 1966.

The *Revised Standard Version of the Bible,* copyrighted 1946 and 1952 was used by permission.

The Pentecostal Movement in the Catholic Church in the U.S.A. was used by permission of Bishop Alexander M. Zaleski, Roman Catholic Diocese, Lansing, Michigan.

FOREWORD

One day in Florida at a luncheon meeting I met the Reverend Robert B. Hall. He spoke on the meaning of the Holy Spirit in his life today. He was alive and filled with the Spirit. "Don't judge me and my words, but do judge by the fruits of the Spirit." I did and they were plentiful.

When I came to Pittsburgh, I met another, the Reverend George W. Stockhowe, and found him bubbling over with the Spirit. His parish church was, too, and all was related to our Lord's life.

The need for personal commitment to our Lord and Saviour Jesus Christ is, as it has ever been, primary in our Christian life. Some Christians may "daily increase in Thy Holy Spirit more and more until he comes unto Thy everlasting kingdom." Others can receive, as Saul did on the road to Damascus, the blinding revelation that Jesus lives.

The spirit of renewal and new life in Christ is very evident in Father Stockhowe's and Joanne's book, and I thank God for them and their witness to the Living Christ.

I especially rejoice in the evidence of the Holy Spirit moving through the several Christian bodies and uniting members of various branches of the Church in this exciting venture. And yet with their common concern and experience, these "new creatures" remain faithful to their own congregations to leaven the loaf and "to work and pray and give for the spread of His Kingdom."

May God bless you and your prayers for these strengthening gifts of the Holy Spirit.

ROBERT B. APPLEYARD, Bishop
Episcopal Diocese of Pittsburgh

FOREWORD

Today the Holy Spirit is blessing many testimonies attesting to the miracle-working power of Jesus Christ among his people. I believe that George Stockhowe's *Jesus Is Alive* is one of those testimonies and that it should find a secure place among the stories which make up the 20th Century book of Acts. It should encourage many Christians who are becoming aware that "Something is happening in the church today," for it is a faithful and inspiring report of what that "Something" is.

DON W. BASHAM

PREFACE

It was just after an ordinary Sunday morning service in January 1971. The ordinary line of people filed by me with their ordinary comments (or silences) on my sermon when along came Dorothy, in the utmost of sincerity, with a very unordinary question. "Father Stockhowe, is it true what I hear that you're holding seances up here during the week?" I, of course, immediately responded with a very emphatic, unqualified, NO! Dorothy left the church that day having willingly taken me at my word and I left the church knowing that indeed the time had come for me to write a book.

Many are the questions that people have been asking about St. Martin's Episcopal Church, Monroeville, Pennsylvania, over the past three years and understandably so. Word seems to have it that something new is going on up here on our hill and, in one sense, that is correct. However, that 'something new' referred to is, in all actuality, just a tremendous awakening of a very old fact established some two thousand years ago—the fact that Jesus is alive!

Just as Luke wrote his gospel to Theophilus (lover of God) to avoid word-of-mouth distortion of the gospel as it had been revealed to him then, so I have

xii

written to avoid distortion of that same gospel as I teach and preach it today. In the words of Luke himself, "It seemed good to me also, having followed all things closely for some time past to write an orderly account for you ... that you may know the truth concerning the things of which you have been informed." Chapter 1:3–4 (RSV)

This, then, is my written account of the people up here on the hill—what we are doing, what we are *not* doing. My earnest prayer is that in reading out story you, too, will come to a greater awakening of the fact that Jesus is alive!

GEORGE W. STOCKHOWE, JR.
St. Martin's Episcopal Church
Monroeville, Pennsylvania

CONTENTS

1. IS HE ALIVE FOR YOU?

"I believe that Jesus died for mankind but not for me."

"I believe in God but not a personal God. Jesus was just a prophet."

"I don't believe Jesus was the Son of God. I see no evidence of it."

The first statement was made to me by a 14-year-old boy who had run away and was found in a bus depot 300 miles from his home. Upon his return he was sent to me and, as we talked, I eventually asked him, "What do you think about Jesus? Do you think He's able to help you with all these problems you have?" That's when he replied, "I believe that Jesus died for mankind but not for me."

The second statement, "I believe in God but not a personal God. Jesus is just another prophet," was made to me by an unmarried teenage girl who had recently had a miscarriage and whose life was further complicated with drugs.

The final statement was made by a layman in his mid-30's who regularly attends our Sunday morning services: a church member yet he doesn't believe Jesus is the Son of God!

Each of these three individuals had come to me in need but none of them were aware of the face that what they really needed was to know that Jesus could be alive for them, too. All of these individuals were members of a Christian church yet religion for each of them was merely a form without any force. Unfortunately, these three aren't the only people I've ever met who feel this way. Their reactions to my question are all too typical of the reactions of countless church-goers who appear Sunday after Sunday in their respective churches, perhaps even actively participating in many of the activities, and yet no one has ever made them aware of the fact that they're missing out on the greatest relationship they can ever have in their life—a personal, daily relationship with Jesus Christ, the Son of God.

If you are one of these people, then let me say to you most emphatically, "Jesus Is Alive!"

"Prove it!" you say? I'm sorry, my friend. I can't do that for you. Nobody can do that for you. I had to prove it for myself and you'll have to prove it for yourself. Does that sound a bit overwhelming to you? Well, it's really not, because if you sincerely want to prove to yourself that Jesus, through the presence of His Holy Spirit, is alive—today—for you, then you're in for a great and glorious adventure. My earnest prayer is that upon reading the adventures in this book, you will want to set out on one of your own.

"I'd like to begin by sharing with you one of my more recent adventures. It was at, of all places, a clergy retreat. Sometimes they are dull, but this one was different. Do you believe that ministers, too, want more of Jesus? They do. It all began when

Gene, an Episcopalian priest, sent the following letter to some of his fellow priests:

February 4, 1971

Dear Friend,

Several of the clergy of the Diocese of Ohio, plus a few brethren from other traditions, plan to meet together on February 17th and 18th in the hope of discovering the Holy Spirit as a greater reality in our lives. We share the realization that it will be only through the Spirit that our ministries will be fruitful; and that without an awareness of His power and presence, more immediate than anything we have yet experienced, our work will increasingly become hollow and superficial.

We expect that those taking part will number about a dozen. While there will be no leader as such, our group will include several persons who have experienced the "Baptism in the Spirit." While the exact agenda or schedule can be determined after we arrive, much time will be given to prayer and sharing.

Baptism in the Holy Spirit. Does that sound strange and unfamiliar to you? When I first heard that phrase, little more than three years ago, it certainly sounded strange to me, so I set out on my own search to find what it was all about. These clergymen from Ohio had heard of my search and its resulting impact on my life and ministry. Wanting to know more about it, they invited me to attend their retreat.

Upon my arrival one snowy afternoon, I was happy to see 13 men had gathered there. The group was composed of nine other Episcopalian priests, one Roman Catholic priest, one Romanian Orthodox priest and two laymen. The two laymen are very active in their work for the Lord. John, a businessman from Elyria, constantly shares his faith with others and holds a weekly prayer meeting in his home. Bob, an English physicist, had come to the United States as a Rotary International Graduate Fellow for 1970–71. He had received the baptism in the Holy Spirit while riding on a mini-bus in Leicester Square, London. Having heard of the meeting he had come seeking felowship.

The format was just as the letter had expressed it—no pre-planned agenda. The afternoon began with singing and prayer. Next there was time for sharing—sharing why we had come, what we were looking for, and the problems and concerns of our own individual lives and ministries. As one priest put it:

"I'm searching for more. I didn't find all the answers in seminary, and I still haven't found all the answers. I have great despair over what is happening to our beloved church. I have heard about this baptism in the Holy Spirit and feel this might be one of the answers. That's why I'm here."

Most of the concerns expressed were similar to this one and were coupled with the desire to have a more personal relationship with Jesus Christ, as some had heard this baptism was supposed to do. It was decided that we would devote the evening to looking at Scripture to see where all this talk about the baptism in the Holy Spirit had come from. Having been the first to suggest this approach, I was elected to lead the Bible study.

Following dinner, we began with prayer and then went into the Scriptures, looking for the phrase "baptism in the Holy Spirit." I pointed out that it first appears in Mark 1:8 . . . "He (Jesus) will baptize you with the Holy Spirit." Discussing the Synoptic Gospels (Matthew, Mark and Luke), I reminded them how we had been taught in seminary that Matthew, Mark and Luke had drawn from various sources in writing their Gospels. It seemed apparent that they all considered this baptism in the Holy Spirit important because each of them referred to it (Matthew 3:11, Luke 3:16). Then the Gospel of John, which is always studied in a different light from the synoptics, also refers to this "baptism in the Holy Spirit." We examined John 1:29–34, where John the Baptist announces three things about Jesus, two of which most Christians are very familiar with. First, ". . . . Here is the Lamb of God who takes away the sin of the world" (John 1:29) and secondly, that "He is the Son of God" (John 1:34). Yet, between these two pronouncements, in John 1:33, we read "He is the one who baptizes with the Holy Spirit." Is not this, too, an essential part of the Good News?

We also looked at our Lord's command to his Apostles in Acts 1:4-5, and then how Peter, once he had seen the Holy Spirit fall upon the Gentiles, recalled that the Lord had said, "John baptized with water but you will be baptized with the Holy Spirit" (Acts 11:16).

Referring to the first disciples, I reminded them

5

how often some clergy and lay people alike remark, "If only I could have lived in the days of Jesus' lifetime! How much easier it would have been to follow Him." Yet on that first Easter night we see that the disciples who had lived with Jesus for three years didn't seem to be having a very easy time of it. John 20:19 tells us "The disciples were gathered together behind locked doors, because they were afraid of the Jews." It wasn't until Pentecost that they were endued with the power of the Holy Spirit and began to witness for Jesus Christ.

We also reviewed some of the many instances in Acts concerning the action of the Holy Spirit and His personal impact. I went on to the references to speaking in tongues, a subject which always raises many questions. Throughout the evening I shared many of my own personal experiences and what had taken place in my parish.

One of the priests suggested we conclude the evening by going upstairs to the chapel for prayer. Another suggested we have specific prayer for anyone desiring to receive the baptism in the Holy Spirit. Of the 14 of us, five clergymen and the two laymen had received this gift prior to this meeting. Three of the clergy now asked some of us to pray with them that they, too, would receive this gift from God.

I think it's interesting to realize that one of the men we prayed with to receive this baptism in the Holy Spirit was the priest who wrote the letter which appears at the beginning of this chapter. "Blessed are those who hunger and thirst for righteousness for they shall be satisfied." (Matthew 5:6 RSV)

The next morning we assembled after breakfast for our last session. We again had a time of sharing and then listened to a tape recording on the Holy Spirit by the Rev. Dennis Bennett, an Episcopalian priest from Seattle, Washington. He has been teaching and preaching on the baptism in the Holy Spirit for over 10 years, not only in his own parish but all over the world as well.

We decided to end our meeting with a celebration of Holy Communion. As we were about to go upstairs to the chapel, Nick, the Orthodox priest, called me aside and asked if we would pray for him to receive the baptism as we had prayed for the others the night before. I responded, "Praise the Lord! It'll be our privilege," and we walked upstairs together.

George, being 60 years old and the eldest of our group, was asked to celebrate the Eucharist. He began the service and then, at the appropriate time in the service for a sermon, he turned to us and said, "No sermon, gentlemen. Just a little homily. I thank God and all of you for the experience of this fellowship ..." That was as far as George could get. He began to choke a little in his deep emotion. He later said, "I'm a hard shell to crack and don't usually show my emotions," but this time in his extreme gratitude he did.

He continued on with the service and when it had ended we began ministering to one another in prayer. We first laid hands on Nick to receive this baptism in the Holy Spirit as he had requested. The infilling of God's Holy Spirit was immediate and he began to speak forth in a new tongue, his new language given to him by the Spirit.

At my request, they then prayed for me that I would be more open and obedient to the guidance of the Holy Spirit in attempting to do God's will. Others asked for prayers as well, all of them primarily for direction in their ministry. George then asked, "Would you pray for me that I might not be so hard-shelled and have so much pride so that God can better use me as He wants?"

We had just finished praying for him when John rather surprisingly asked, "Is there anyone here who has a back problem?"

"Why yes," Nick responded, "I've had much trouble involving a lot of pain at times."

"Well," John continued, "oftentimes back problems are related to a difference in length in an individual's legs. It has been estimated that over 70% of us have one leg shorter than the other."

There was a momentary silence. John then went on to say that he thought we should pray for Nick's leg to be lengthened since that could possibly be the cause of his back trouble. I agreed with John and told them I, too, had seen this miracle of leg lengthening several times just recently.

"Yes," Arthur added, "I had mine miraculously lengthened just about a year ago."

Nick sat down in a chair and we all gathered around him. As he straightened out his legs, it was very obvious that one was at least one-half inch shorter than the other. John and I supported his legs as John prayed for them to be made equal in length. Immediately, before our eyes, Nick's short leg grew out to become even with the other. We had witnessed a miracle and our faith was further deepened. I met Nick at a conference seven weeks later. He was anxious to report that he has had no pain in his back since the retreat.

Our little group had been together less than 24 hours but through it God had once again assured us that He will act when we seek Him! One of the priests made the comment that in all the clergy meetings and conferences he had ever attended, this was the first time that brother priests had ministered to one another in prayer on such a personal basis. The others agreed. We each returned to our respective parishes that afternoon refreshed and more aware than ever that Jesus is alive. But I'm getting ahead of my story . . .

2. SEEK AND YOU WILL FIND

"And it shall come to pass afterward, that I will pour out my spirit on all flesh; . . . Even upon the menservants and maidservants in those days will I pour out my spirit." (Joel 2:28–29 RSV)

Little did I believe, even as recently as three years ago, that this prophecy of Joel was to become such a reality in my life and in the lives of countless others.

The Holy Spirit has been with us most assuredly at St. Martin's since our inception in 1955 when about a dozen interested families and I stepped out in faith to begin holding services as a brand-new mission of the Episcopal Diocese of Pittsburgh. We met in a dilapidated, 50-year-old community house, and, only four months out of seminary, I found myself preaching from a pulpit which consisted of three pop cases covered with a sheet. Since that time, we've grown to the status of a parish with facilities whose material value now totals over one-half million dollars. Yet it was not until the spring of 1968 that some of the men and women of our congregation became more fully aware of this promise of the outpouring of the Holy Spirit.

As a thriving, young, suburban parish for 12

years previous to that spring, we had placed the bulk of our efforts in establishing our material assets and, as the pastor of this flock, most of my time had been consumed in building and equipping the church plant. Many of us had been growing spiritually as well, in spite of the fact that in my preaching I had placed little emphasis on the need for a personal encounter with Jesus Christ. In fact, as one of my parishioners recently reminded me, most of my sermons in those previous years seemed to deal more with psychology and sex than with Jesus Christ. Perhaps she was right. But I do remember preaching a series of six sermons on salvation in February and March of 1964. I remember because of a letter my wife, Joanne, sent to me after I had preached the first five sermons in that series.

Although she had grown up in the Episcopal Church and had been faithful and active in it since childhood, prior to that March of 1964 she had never made any definite personal commitment to Jesus Christ. Through a series of circumstances that developed that winter, she began to realize this.

A minister and his wife from Canada spent an evening with us in December 1963. Joanne had never met any couple so enthusiastic in their conversation about the Lord and began to realize they had something she didn't have. Unfortunately, we were never to see them again, once they left our house that night, but they had kindled a spark and Joanne suddenly developed an interest in "religious" books. One of her favorites at the time was *With the Holy Spirit and with Fire* by the late Dr. Samuel S. Shoemaker. In addition, when Lent started in February, she began attending our Wednesday morning School of Prayer lectures given by Muriel, one of our own parishioners. Muriel had given the same lectures two years earlier but Joanne wasn't interested then and only attended one session. Now, however, her spiritual hunger was such that she didn't want to miss even one.

Then, one Tuesday night in March 1964, she was standing at our kitchen sink washing dishes. As she did, a tremendous feeling of love came over her and then it became so intense that she left the kitchen and came into the living room where I was half asleep on the sofa. She tried to explain to me just how she was feeling, hoping all the while that I wouldn't think she was just being ridiculous and laugh it off. Then she had the courage to ask what sounded almost absurd as she thought about it, yet what was foremost on her mind:

"Do you think all this love I'm feeling could be the Holy Spirit like Sam Shoemaker tells about in his book?"

"Could be!" I replied.

As she now relates it, "As soon as he said that, this overwhelming feeling of love grew even more intense and I knew then it had to be the Holy Spirit. All I wanted to do was pray and yet, somehow, I really couldn't find the right words."

About a half hour later I had to leave for a dinner meeting. Just before I did, Joanne came up to the bedroom where I was looking for my cuff links.

"Will you pray with me before you leave?" she asked.

Now that may not sound like such an unusual request, considering that it came from a minister's wife, but it was actually most unusual. We had rarely ever prayed together, except at meals, but by now I was aware that what was happening to her was very real and beautiful and of God. We got down on our knees together at our bed and I thanked Him for this glorious revelation of Jesus Christ in her life.

The next day was Wednesday and she went to our regular weekly service of Holy Communion. As she knelt to receive the bread and wine, this sense of love, which had never left since the night before when she first became aware of it, became more intense than ever and she could only pray, "Lord, I don't know what you want to do with me, but whatever it is, take me and use me!"

After the service she left the church, having spoken little to anyone. She was still much too caught up in the wonder of those past 24 hours to be able to share what had been happening to her.

Four days later, on Saturday morning, she sat down and wrote me the following letter, using an anonymous approach because she didn't think it was necessary for the congregation at that time to know who had written it. Consequently, I'm sure no one was as moved as I was the next morning when I read it to the congregation at the conclusion of my sermon.

Saturday, March 7, 1964

Dear Mr. Stockhowe,
Since the opportunity to speak with you hasn't come yet due to our conflicting schedules, I have

decided to write this rather than to have to express myself over the phone.

About six weeks ago my husband and I entertained a business acquaintance and his wife from out of town. The evening was a pleasant one, but uneventful until well after midnight, when somehow our conversation turned to the church. Almost immediately our guests began to monopolize the conversation and my husband and I sat almost speechless as we listened to them tell that they had not really come to know God until their early 30s, in spite of having been regular church-goers since childhood. Then they went on to tell us some of the unbelievable changes that have since been taking place in their lives.

To go into detail in this letter is unnecessary. It is sufficient to say that as they spoke, it became obvious to me that in spite of my life-long membership in the church I did not really know God. It is difficult to explain but I'm sure you will understand when I say that these guests prompted a burning sensation within me which, as I have come to know this past week, was the Holy Spirit. For the previous six weeks I had been living with an off-again, on-again smoldering within me (both physical and mental). I tried to cast it off as "mere emotion" but at the same time I wasn't really sure I wanted to cast it off. Then last Wednesday as I received Holy Communion, I felt the *real* presence of Christ for the first time in my life and this smoldering which I'd had burst into flame and I left the church as a new person.

I thought I would burst as I waited for my husband to come home and after I'd told him of my experiences we knelt together and thanked God for this tremendous revelation of Jesus Christ.

There are no words to describe what has happened

14

to me in these past four days. I am convinced you know of what I speak, else you wouldn't have spent these past five Sundays preaching about conversion. And this finally brings me to my main purpose in writing to you.

Forgive me for being presumptuous, but having listened intently to these recent sermons of yours, I feel that you are no doubt planning another sermon on the same subject for tomorrow.

If this is the case, will you please tell the congregation that you know of at least one of them that has been converted just this past week? Tell them you know someone who has gloriously come to realize what you have so earnestly and sincerely spoken of in recent weeks.

Tell them that I actually fought a battle with the Holy Spirit for six weeks and that I so very fortunately lost out to Him at the altar last Wednesday. Tell them of the profound sense of joy I felt as I related my new birth first to my husband, then to a dear friend and now to you.

Tell them also that for the first time in my life I lay awake until the wee hours of Thursday morning, overpowered by the almost unbelievable events of the day and how I still awoke well before the alarm, refreshed and anxious to begin another day.

Tell them I was too overjoyed to eat for the first time in my life. And tell them that for the first time in my life I got down on my knees and prayed because I *wanted* to pray.

Tell them that Christ was as real to me last Friday as I scrubbed the dirty kitchen floor as He had been on Wednesday at the altar.

Tell them as I related my joy to my husband that I found a new depth of love and understanding be-

15

tween us and tell them as I shared my joy with my dear friend, I had my first taste of true friendship.

Tell them it was easy to refrain from cursing the bedboard as I painfully hit my shin against it, and tell them that until last week, to pray was a real chore and when I did, it was usually for my immediate family. Tell them that in two days my prayer list grew to over 100 names and it will continue to grow.

Also tell them not to look around expecting to see someone in their midst with a halo or wings. The only real difference in me since last Sunday is my reason for coming. Last week I went to church because I've been told all my life it's the right thing to do. Tomorrow I will be there because I sincerely want to be.

If you should choose to tell your people these things, please emphasize to them that I realize that in the days, weeks, months, and years to come all will *not* be as painless as these past four days have been.

I know there will be times of despair and disappointment and grief and that situations will arise which will seem hopeless. There will be burdens to bear and frightening decisions to be made. God alone knows what lies before me to do or to suffer, but because I have now honestly and sincerely accepted Him into my life I am not afraid of what tomorrow may bring.

I *know* that my Redeemer lives!"

As she had predicted in her letter, the following months and years were not as painless as those first four days of her new life in Christ had been. Over the next four years, she gradually fell away from her personal prayer routine and the "religious" books and the Bible became less and less a part of her life.

By the winter of 1968 she had reached an all-time spiritual low.

It was in February of that same year that I began to see what a great need there was for more spiritual depth in our church. About 30 of our men and women had begun meeting for the first of a series of discussions titled, "Growing in the Faith." In order to introduce the first session, I asked the question: "What is a Christian?" and we had little problem agreeing that a Christian was someone who had accepted Jesus Christ as his Lord and Savior.

This led to my next question: "What does it mean to accept Jesus Christ as your Lord and Savior?" That proved to be a rather embarrassing challenge to those present, some of the most faithful in the church. Three sessions later found them still struggling for an answer on which they could all agree and found me seriously questioning just how much of a spiritual father I had actually been to these people.

To further complicate the situation, I was more concerned than ever about Joanne. She now had no desire to pray, or even talk about church or the Lord. I had encouraged her to attend these sessions, hoping that through them she would find some spark of encouragement that would erase at least some of her doubts and help to revive her now wavering faith.

Unfortunately, after three consecutive weeks of hearing some of our most respected people flounder over "What does it mean to accept Jesus Christ as your Lord and Savior?" her doubts turned to sheer unbelief and each meeting proved to be more of a setback for her. Finally, she readily admitted to me one evening in mid-February that she could no longer see any value in attending church. She told me she had just finished reading an article in *Time* magazine on the "God is dead" movement and was inclined to agree that He was. As her husband, and knowing all the circumstances that led to her present state of affairs, there was little I could do but pray that soon she would somehow be reawakened to the loving hand of Jesus in her life.

Prior to these study sessions, late in the summer of 1967, a curious set of seemingly unrelated circumstances began to develop in my own life. As I now view them, in retrospect, I know without a doubt that it was the Holy Spirit guiding me into and through each of them.

As I was browsing through Westminster bookstore downtown one morning, I met Paul, a very dedicated Christian friend, for whom I had much respect and admiration. In the course of our conversation, he reached into one rack and handed me a copy of John L. Sherrill's book, *They Speak with Other Tongues*. He said only:

"That's interesting reading. There's a lot to it."

"I'm sure it is," I responded. Then, without even opening it, I put it right back on the rack as we continued our conversation.

It was almost Thanksgiving before Paul and I met again. He had come to a Sunday morning service and I invited him to have lunch with me later that week. He accepted and I looked forward to the privilege of meeting and sharing with him once again. I don't remember all that transpired over our lunch

18

that day, but I do remember that it was then he first mentioned his association with a group of college students from Duquesne University. He explained that they met for prayer every Friday night in one of the students' homes on Mt. Washington and invited me to attend a meeting with him. Again, I was relatively unimpressed, just as I had been with his suggestion that I read Sherrill's book; however, out of my deep respect for him, I did agree to join him at one of these meetings soon after the Christmas holidays.

My deep respect for Paul—why else would I bother to drive across the city on that cold January night? These students were, first of all, strangers and, secondly, Roman Catholic, so I wondered whether their meeting would be a waste of time for me. When I arrived the session had already begun, and my first reaction was one of utter amazement. There must have been at least 20 students crowded into the humble, poorly furnished living room, praising the Lord in songs which stunned me by their informality and exuberance. The beautiful freedom with which they sang carried over into their prayers which followed:

"Thank you, Jesus, for the words you gave me to speak to Susan this morning."

"Thank you, Jesus."

"How we love you."

"Praise your holy name!"

Intermittently, the prayers would cease as someone would begin to share some way in which Jesus had been especially alive in his or her life during the past week. Woven throughout the entire meeting

19

were spontaneous Scripture readings from various students. These assorted passages obviously were not prepared and chosen in advance, but always seemed to emerge most appropriately from the conversation as they shared with one another. This was a major revelation for me. Never had I known of any Roman Catholic anywhere (or Episcopalian) who had the desire to read the Bible that these young people had. Also, from time to time, someone would begin to pray in a foreign language and I assumed these were the tongues my friend Paul had wanted me to read about.

What mixed emotions I took home with me that night! Never had I seen anything like that before. How tremendous it was to see them so freely and beautifully exalting Jesus Christ, and to see them continually turning to Scripture for their inspiration and guidance. There was such an abundance of love for the Lord as well as for one another, but what about those different languages they spoke? What good was there in praying in words no one else could understand? While I doubted the necessity for their "tongues," I was still very deeply touched by the extreme sincerity of their worship and left their meeting that night realizing that somehow Jesus was much more alive to these students than He was to me.

It was also about this time that I became annoyed with Muriel. She and her husband had now been parishioners for almost five years. She had composed her School of Prayer lectures in thanksgiving to God for some very special blessings in her life. After giving the lectures twice at St. Martin's, she had now been asked to present them in churches all over the city. Through her love and simplicity, countless women were being brought closer to the Lord. She had been a wonderful asset to my ministry. I always had the utmost respect for her and her sincere devotion to our Lord, but it seemed to me that lately she was placing entirely too much emphasis on the need for an individual to have some definite personal experience with Jesus. This, I felt, was leaning much too far toward emotionalism and when she stopped by my office one morning in November 1967, I told her so in no uncertain terms. Thereafter, for week upon week, we found ourselves deliberately evading one another.

Then, one day in late January, she phoned for an appointment with me. When she arrived the following Thursday, she suggested we go in the church to talk and she began by saying, "I wanted this opportunity to talk because I just don't want to go on being separated from my priest like this." We began to share once again, and, as we did, it became apparent that our relationship was being restored.

She must have considered it very solidly restored, or else she wouldn't have had the courage to say what she did upon leaving:

"I'm going to Kathryn Kuhlman's healing service again tomorrow. Why don't you come along?"

While given the boldness to make such a request, I'm sure she expected to hear a firm, "No!" in response, but by now I had seen and heard just enough to know that I would have to see and hear more—even Kathryn Kuhlman—before I would be able to come to any more definite conclusions. I doubt that Muriel will ever entirely recover from her initial shock when, without any hesitation, I agreed to go with her that very next morning.

The service was not to start until 11 o'clock, but when we arrived just after 10, the only available seats were in the balcony. Like many first-time visitors, I had brought with me several preconceived notions. First, I was certain that the majority of the congregation would be poorly dressed, poorly educated, and extremely emotional people who would thereby be excellent subjects for what I suspected must be Miss Kuhlman's high-powered chicanery. To my amazement, this was not the case at all. Although her method of worship was unlike my own, it was obvious that what I witnessed here was not a result of any of Miss Kuhlman's own manufactured high spirits, but very definitely the work of the Holy Spirit of God. Furthermore, while many had come from a low economic background, just as many, if not more, were there from the upper middle-class bracket. Numerous people were visibly healed that day and when the service ended about 2 o'clock, I went away realizing that the major ingredient of that service was expectancy. Those people had gone there expecting that Jesus, through His Holy Spirit, would be there moving in their midst and would heal. Why didn't my people come to my services with similar expectancy? It gave me much food for thought and urged me to continue on in my investigation.

3. JOANNE JOINS
THE SEARCH

Joanne had been substituting at the high school the day I went to Kathryn Kuhlman's. When I picked her up after school, we exchanged the usual greetings and I asked her how her day had gone, hoping she'd ask me about mine. But she didn't. To force the issue, I had to come out bluntly with, "I'll bet you'll never guess where I went today."

"Nothing would surprise me!" she replied.

When I told her, it did surprise her. Her first response was, "Did you wear your collar?"

"Of course, I wore my collar," I said. "Who should I have been afraid of?"

I went on to give a blow-by-blow account, not really very sure of just how it was affecting her. She seemed to be interested at first, but at one point when I stopped my rambling momentarily, she got a word in.

"So what else is new?" she asked.

I dropped the subject for the time being.

As I explained in the last chapter, she was experiencing at this time one of the longest and driest spiritual periods I had ever known her to have. I could only pray that in some way she would soon have her faith restored. Then, one Sunday after church in early February, as we were having lunch, I just happened to mention that lately a few of the women from St. Martin's had been to Tibb's prayer group in her home in Mt. Lebanon and were very much impressed. That did it! Up to now she had always listened each time I would share these things with her, even though I knew her attitude was generally, "I'll go my way, you go yours!" This time it was different. She immediately exploded.

"First the Duquesne group, then Kathryn Kuhlman and now Tibb's! It's too bad those women can't find something more constructive to do than run to prayer meetings for spiritual kicks—and you don't seem any better! I get more disgusted every time I hear you. What's Tibb got that we haven't got?"

"Why don't you go find out for yourself?" I replied. "Then, and only then, will you be able to justly criticize. Until then, don't!"

Just a few weeks later, Joanne and Ellie, a college friend of hers, had made arrangements to have lunch with Pat, another college friend, in Mt. Lebanon. Since they weren't meeting Pat until 12:30, Joanne asked Ellie, a life-long Presbyterian, if she would mind leaving home early so they could visit a prayer group she had heard so much about. Ellie agreed and off they went, neither knowing quite what to expect. Joanne had phoned some of our own women who had been there before to make sure it wasn't a group where she would have to pray out loud herself. They all were most emphatic about the fact that the people there only spoke or prayed when they chose to and that they probably wouldn't even ask her name because the group was so large. That suited her fine because she really wasn't looking forward to going. She knew, as I did, that she was going mainly so she could come home and be "justly critical." However, the day proved to be an answer to many of my prayers for her spiritual welfare. I'll let her explain it in her own words.

"Ellie and I had no trouble finding Tibb's house or parking, so we arrived about 20 minutes early (much earlier than I had intended) and were greeted at the door by a woman who seemed much too striking to be the 'prayer-group type.' She very graciously welcomed us and then proceeded to record our names and the church we attended. Blow number one—I was on their list! Ellie didn't seem to care, but then she hadn't come with a chip on her shoulder as I had. My next maneuver was to quickly find a seat and sit down before I had to speak to anyone else. Since several rows of folding chairs had been placed in the dining room, we walked out there and as I went to sit down I picked up the song book on my chair. Blow number two—the title on the cover read 'Camp Farthest Out' and all I could think was, It sure is!

"I tried to appear casual to Ellie so she wouldn't feel too uncomfortable, but I was getting more uncomfortable by the minute and wished I'd never come. At last 10 o'clock came. By now the living room and dining room were filled with at least 60 women and one minister, Rev. Russ Bixler, from the Church of the Brethren in Pittsburgh.

"Tibb called everyone to order and said, 'We usually open our meeting with a scripture reading, but I just feel such a heaviness here this morning that I think instead we should begin by going around the room having each one of you thank God for something special He's done in your life this week.' Blow of all blows! I should pray in front of these people? Those women back home assured me I wouldn't have to pray. I'd been framed! There wasn't even a back door to slip through. Then I thought of poor Ellie. I got her into this and now she was going to have to say a prayer to get out. What a mess I'd gotten us into!

"Fortunately, there must have been at least 40 prayers ahead of us, so I had time to think one up. I finally decided that when my turn came I could probably say, "Thank you God for the privilege of being here today.' Rather a two-faced prayer, but at least it would sound respectable and get me off the hook. Then I realized that, because of the way we were sitting, Ellie would have to pray first. Poor Ellie; I dared not even look in her direction. Then along came blow number four. It was Ellie's turn now and she prayed such a lovely, flowing prayer that I would have rather died than be next. When she had finished, I mustered up enough strength to blurt out, "Thank you, God, for the privilege of being here today.' Then I breathed a deep sigh of relief. That was one more obstacle out of the way and I began to wonder how else they could possibly threaten me. Much to my satisfaction, however, the remainder of the meeting proved to be really quite harmless.

"After joining in on a few of those Camp Farthest

26

Out songs, I realized they really weren't too far out, nor were the people who so freely shared their experiences and concerns and were so quick to offer their loving individual prayers as the need arose. Many prayers just praised God for being God. While I never did completely relax all morning, by the time noon arrived, I was almost enjoying myself. These women exhibited so much love that they seemed to actually enjoy being religious! If I truly did have a chip on my shoulder when I entered her house that morning, then Tibb must have had to sweep it off her dining room floor that afternoon because I had no chip on my way out—only a very deep sense that what I'd seen and heard there was something very beautiful and real. I talked with Tibb just last week and reminded her of my first visit to her group. She told me that in the 15 years it's been since she started it, only once did she ever request that everyone in the group offer a prayer. That, of course, was on the day Ellie and I went there. Interesting, isn't it?"

I praise God for leading Joanne to Tibb's meeting that day. Among other things, it served to rekindle that spark within her and thereafter *my* search became *ours*.

Our first venture together was to attend a Friday night dinner meeting of the Full Gospel Businessmen's Fellowship International. That's FGBMFI for short. This organization of Christian businessmen sponsors an open dinner meeting once each month at a local restaurant. The dinner is always followed by an address from some visiting speaker and we had heard that the speaker at this February meeting would be the Rev. James Brown, a Presbyterian minister from Parkesburg, Pennsylvania.

As we walked in the door of the restaurant we were greeted with an exuberant, "Hello, brother," and "Hello, sister," by two men standing near the coat racks. Now, "Father" I was used to, but to be addressed as "brother" was almost funny—as was "sister" to Joanne. The warmth and sincerity of these men, however, far exceeded any humor we found in their unfamiliar terminology.

We sat down at one of the long banquet tables to find ourselves in the immediate company of one Methodist, two Roman Catholics, two Presbyterians, and two Episcopalian's, all from different areas of the city. Just the dinner conversation alone was well worth going for. Once again, I found myself in the midst of a group of people who delighted in talking about their faith in Jesus Christ, as did the speaker, Jim Brown. He held everyone's attention for well over 90 minutes with one story after another that revealed God's hand in his own life as well as the lives of others. He preached to an overflow crowd that must have numbered over 600, but no one looked at his watch. As Jim concluded with prayer, one man spoke a message in an unknown language, which was then interpreted by another and I explained to Joanne this was the gift of tongues I had been telling her about. Those desiring special prayer for salvation or the baptism in the Holy Spirit were asked to go to another room. As might be expected, we both were still much too reluctant—or should I say proud—to avail ourselves of the opportunity.

The last two weeks of March that year found

Joanne going off to her parents in Florida with our three boys. Because of the coming Holy Week services, I stayed behind. This left little time to go on searching, but I did send Joanne on her way with a copy of *They Speak with Other Tongues*, hoping she would find time to read it amidst the clamor of our three overactive sons. Somehow she managed to finish it on the train on the way down, and here's what she wrote me upon reaching Florida:

I read every word of Sherrill's book. I didn't want to put it down but whenever I had to, I made sure I covered it up with something so no one on the train would see the title and think I'd flipped. Oh, George, I know we both need this baptism he writes about. I'm sure of that now and can't wait to get home so we can find out more about it.

Imagine all that in one letter—and without my husbandly encouragement. It was hard for me to believe this was the same wife who six weeks earlier was rebelling at some of her women friends and accusing them of only being out for spiritual kicks. How gloriously the Lord was continuing to answer my prayers for her.

When she returned home, I took her with me to one of the Duquesne prayer meetings. While most anxious to go, she was still a bit nervous and ill at ease in the meeting one of the girls spoke a most beautiful prophecy.

"Fear not, my daughter, I love you . . . ," she began. The words of encouragement continued, but neither of us remember what they all were. At the time,

Joanne knew little about the gift of prophecy and didn't recognize it as such. Somehow, though, she knew this was truly the Lord speaking His words of comfort to her through another individual. I watched her gradually relax and become more a part of the group as the evening progressed. When the time came for intercessions, my heart was suddenly warmed as she very audibly and beautifully offered her own personal prayer requests—another meeting and another answer to my prayers for her. Praise His Wonderful Name!

4. ASK AND YOU WILL RECEIVE

It was early May 1968 and by now we had both seen and heard enough to make us look forward to the first annual conference on the Holy Spirit which was to be held that month in Pittsburgh. The kick-off dinner was limited to clergy and their wives and members of religious communities. Over 400 attended that Monday night to hear men from each of three different denominations give their testimonies. Two were ministers, one Anglican (Episcopalian) and one Presbyterian, and one was a Roman Catholic student from Notre Dame. After hearing them speak, both of us knew we definitely wanted to be at the seminary the next day for the first day of the conference.

Anxious as we were, we were still much too proud to let anyone else know exactly how we felt. Throughout the first two days of lectures we desperately tried to maintain the role of casual observers, but it was a losing battle right from the very start.

We almost never arrive on time anywhere for anything, but somehow we found ourselves 30 minutes early for the first meeting on Tuesday morning. At the entrance of the chapel we saw Russ. Joanne immediately recognized him as the minister from the Church of the Brethren who had sat all through Tibb's prayer meeting that day looking so disgustingly happy. Seeing my clerical collar, he introduced himself and asked me to join him for prayer with the clergy who would be leading the conference. Then, being careful not to leave Joanne feeling unnecessary, he picked up a handful of programs from the table and said, "Will you please give one of these to each person who comes in the door?" How could she refuse? She spent the next half hour very officially giving directions and handing out programs while I, just as officially, prayer with Russ and the conference leaders. Some casual observers we turned out to be!

When the first session was about to begin, I returned to the chapel and Joanne and I intended to slip unobtrusively into one of the back rows. But the only plugs for my tape recorder were in the very first rows by the piano. Determined to get all these teachings on tape, we had no choice but to go forward and take seats in the very first row—another very inappropriate position for two casual observers.

While I was setting up my recorder, Joanne pointed out several of our women parishioners as they came in. Out of the seven women and one man who had come, only one had not already been baptized in the Holy Spirit and we knew it. This fact was much more annoying to Joanne than to me, and throughout the next three days she continually referred to them as the "breathers." She said she knew they were all just going to "breathe down our backs" until we got this baptism in the Holy Spirit.

It was the one male breather that I found myself annoyed by. He was Milton, a very well-respected man from my congregation, whose only major fault in my eyes was that he was just a little too spiritually minded for my satisfaction. Somehow, I always felt much more comfortable when he wasn't around.

We heard speaker upon speaker that day—morning, afternoon, and evening, Baptist, Presbyterian, Anglican, and Roman Catholic. One of our most vivid recollections was that of seeing the handsome Roman Catholic student from Notre Dame standing in the pulpit of that Presbyterian chapel accompanying himself on his guitar while he led us all in singing, "We Are One in the Spirit, We Are One in the Lord." What a deeply moving scene it was for everyone there.

My mother had agreed to move in with our boys and we were delighted because this meant Joanne could attend every session if she so desired and she did. We could feel the momentum of the conference building session by session, and by Wednesday afternoon we had reached some very definite conclusions:

1. We were going to have prayer for the baptism in the Holy Spirit.
2. We would ask the Anglican priest to pray for us, but it would be privately.
3. This was going to be our own little thing, and we weren't going to tell anyone even after we had received the baptism.

I cornered the Anglican priest that same afternoon before dinner and asked if he would meet with us for a few minutes of prayer before that evening's session. I did not specify that we desired prayer for the baptism in the Holy Spirit, but he very kindly agreed. Seven-thirty that same night found the three of us seated at a table in a small office. We began with a few questions we had on our minds and then he said, "Now let's have a prayer before we leave." He proceeded to pray very generally that we would be guided and directed by the Spirit, and then, having finished, got up to be on his way. We were both crushed. Both of us had come earnestly desiring prayer for the baptism in the Holy Spirit, but nowhere in the course of the short conversation did either of us have the courage to come right out and tell him so. How else could he have known our specific intentions?

The address that evening was to be given by that same Anglican priest and I had suggested to the men from our Brotherhood of St. Andrew that they should come and bring their wives. About six couples accepted my invitation. As we entered the fellowship hall, we could see them scattered here and there around the room. When the speaker concluded his most inspiring message, he announced that for those who wished to stay there would be opportunity for personal prayer. He instructed those who desired prayer for healing to come to the front of the hall and those who desired prayer for the baptism in the Holy Spirit to exit out the side door into the chapel.

By this time, Joanne was so strongly convicted that she knew she couldn't leave that night without having prayer for the baptism in the Holy Spirit, but the side door was on the far side of the room and she was well aware how conspicuous it would be to move in that direction. To exit to the chapel would in effect be announcing publicly that she wanted the baptism. At this point she was not nearly as concerned about the "breathers" as she was about the men from our Brotherhood and their wives. Most of them were attending the conference for the first time that night and would have little or no understanding of this baptism. How would it affect these people to see their minister's wife heading for the chapel? Then it occurred to her that if she really and truly was looking for more of the Lord by taking this step, then walking through that "labeled" door was such a very small price to pay.

I was busy gathering up my tape recording apparatus when she came over to me.

"I'm going over to the chapel now," she said. "Where should I meet you after?"

"Wait a minute," I replied, "I'm going too." And off we "casual observers" went to the chapel for prayer.

We arrived there to find not the Anglican but the Presbyterian and Baptist ministers in charge. We were asked to sit every other row so that they could eventually come and minister to us individually. There must have been 35 to 40 other men and women scattered through the chapel that night. The Presbyterian minister led us in group prayer, asking that each of us be baptized in the Holy Spirit. Then he and the Baptist minister and several laymen began to circulate throughout the pews praying for people individually. Joanne and I knelt there in silent prayer while others around us began to experience some very audible manifestations. Some sobbed, some murmured "Thank you, Jesus," some shouted "Hallelujah!" while many others burst forth in their newly received tongues. Neither of us were experiencing any outward signs but then we didn't particularly want to.

We must have knelt there five minutes. I still had my head bowed and eyes closed when I felt a hand on my shoulder and I looked up. There before me stood Milton. My first immediate prayer was, "Lord, not Milton! Anybody—but not Milton!" But then he proceeded to lay hands on both of us and pray a beautiful prayer for us and our ministry at St. Martin's and then quietly slipped away.

The Presbyterian minister came by to gently encourage us to begin speaking in tongues, but we were still much too inhibited by the entire situation to respond. "You do the speaking, you do the speaking," he repeated again and again. "The Holy Spirit never forces Himself on anyone—you have to begin to speak."

Each of us, unknown at the time to the other, did begin to whisper a few syllables. Then feeling rather ridiculous, we immediately sealed our lips once again. Many were still there in prayer when we left but we saw no need to stay any longer oursleves. As before, we passed through the rear door to the hall and found ourselves face to face with three "breathers" standing in the rear of the chapel. To keep from disturbing those still there in prayer, we just shook their hands and smiled as we went on by. Joanne has said many times since, "We left the chapel that night with such an abundance of joy and peace and love within us that I even enjoyed saying goodnight to the breathers!"

As we began walking across the seminary campus to the car, I said to Joanne, "You're disappointed in a way, aren't you?"

"A little, I guess!" she replied. Then we both began to laugh.

"Do you know why we're disappointed?" I asked. "Because we've been wanting this baptism in the Holy Spirit so much, and yet we've been trying to tell the Lord exactly how we are going to get it. We're disappointed tonight because we didn't receive as we *thought* we were going to receive. We weren't as expressive as some of the others around us because neither of us *chose* to be that expressive. But we've asked for the gift and we've received, and we shouldn't be disappointed because we didn't react emotionally the way some of these others did. Just praise the Lord for this wonderful new blessing in our lives!"

By now we had reached the car and as we drove away, Joanne spoke.

"Did you get any words in a new language?"

"Only two or three syllables, but they didn't make sense so I quit. How about you?"

"Well," she said, "when he told me just to speak out anything I whispered one word, 'golomb,' and I immediately thought, 'that's the paint and glass company they advertise on TV,' so I didn't try anymore either."

At this, we both broke into a roar of laughter that continued almost uncontrollably all the way home.

When we stopped for a red light near the Churchill Police Station, I felt uneasy—if an officer had come over to our car he would have hauled us both in for a sobriety test. Even after we arrived home, we continued to laugh on into the night.

We didn't realize it at the time, but just as tears or hallelujahs had been a release for some of those people back in the chapel, so laughter had been a release for us. The overflow of joy which comes to an individual upon receiving the baptism in the Holy Spirit manifests itself in various ways. We are not the only ones ever to express this joy through laughter. We have since met numerous people who have had the same manifestation. The Lord works in marvelous ways His wonders to perform.

We spent the remainder of the week resting up from our glorious but exhausting conference. Busy months of searching had climaxed when we asked for and received this gift of the Holy Spirit. There remained one more question to be resolved, however, and that concerned the business of tongues. After hearing much teaching we felt this, too, was a gift for everyone just as is the baptism in the Holy Spirit and would be a most valuable aid to our spiritual growth, but we still could not pray in the language of the Holy Spirit.

The following Monday, I attended my first meeting of a group of ministers from all denominations, most of whom had already received the baptism in the Holy Spirit. When the meeting was over, there was time for individual ministry to one another. I asked for special prayer, explaining that perhaps I didn't receive the baptism in the Holy Spirit the previous week because I could not yet speak in tongues. Several of the clergy gathered around to pray and, as they did, one of the men encouraged me to speak out whatever came to my lips. As I did, several new words came out and a sensation I can describe only as a warm coolness came over my body. I began to speak a few words in the language of the Spirit and they all began thanking the Lord for my newly received gift of tongues.

I went upstairs to phone Joanne to see if she needed anything from the store, but I chose not to tell her what had just happened. My next stop was the supermarket, and as I wheeled the shopping cart down the first aisle, the Spirit began to well up within me. I felt a strong desire to praise God in my newly given language. No one else was aware of what I was doing because I never spoke above a whisper, but for the next 15 minutes I pushed my cart up and down the aisles praising God in a new tongue.

It was not until about six weeks later that Joanne received her language in an entirely different way. Before going to bed one night that June, she had played a tape by David DuPlessis concerning the nature of the gift of tongues and how to receive it. Several times during the night she awakened to find herself speaking words she'd never heard before. The next morning as she prayed alone in her bedroom, her new language flowed forth and she was then moved to begin singing these new words as well.

Our search was over and now I began to wonder, "Where do we go from here?"

5. WHAT WILL THE BISHOP SAY?

Soon after coming into this new-found experience, my desire was to speak to my spiritual Father in God, who at that time was Bishop Austin Pardue. I knew him to be a man with deep spiritual insight. I wanted to know what he would think of my personal involvement, and just whether or not he would permit me to preach my convictions to my people.

Off I went to the Diocesan offices, and found the bishop had a few free minutes. Sitting beside his desk, I began my story telling him of my search and my experience. He listened very intently.

"Bishop," I said, "I want to preach about this. I want to share it with others, and I want your advice and opinion before I do."

He sat back in his chair and replied, "George, I don't doubt your spiritual experience. However, let me warn you, as I have warned other clergy who have become involved in various religious movements. You will certainly attract the 5% or 10% of the people who are often classified as the neurotic, psychotic or emotionally disturbed. These are the people who will cause you the most problems. They will be the ones, more than any others, who will misquote and misguide. But remember, Jesus loves them and so must you. It's very possible you may be able to help them. Continue to share your experiences with your people. Let me know how it goes. If you need me, I'm here. God bless you!"

I felt greatly encouraged as I left his office that morning. My Bishop had given me his blessing.

It was only a few months later that Bishop Pardue retired from the Diocese of Pittsburgh and was replaced by Bishop Appleyard. I wanted very much to go and see my new spiritual leader and seek his guidance. When the opportunity presented itself to meet with him, I did, putting everything "above board" with all honesty and openness. I told him what I had done, what I hoped to do, and what I was preaching in my parish. Then I was ready for the big question.

"What do you think, Bishop?"

"George," he replied, "I thank you for sharing this with me. I believe there is a place for all of this in the Church. I trust you. Do continue to keep me informed of any new developments."

These were wonderful words of reassurance—"I trust you." Coming from his lips, I knew they were more than mere words. I asked to be relieved of my position as Chairman of the Department of Youth in the Diocese, feeling that a younger priest, more closely associated with youth, could better serve in this capacity. I had already served as chairman for seven years, but he asked me to serve another year until he could better get the feel of his new diocese. I followed his wishes, often reminding him of my resignation during that year. He finally appointed my successor, but the very same day, to my complete surprise, he appointed me Chairman of the Department of Evangelism in the diocese. Thus, I was further assured of his confidence and trust in me and my ministry.

More and more clergy are coming into this experience and then looking to their spiritual denominational leaders for guidance and direction. Two denominations, the Roman Catholics and Presbyterians, after serious study and investigation, have published their findings to help their clergy and laypeople.

Following are portions from the text of a report, "The Pentecostal Movement in the Catholic Church in the U.S.A.", submitted to the semi-annual meeting of the U.S. Catholic Bishops in Washington, D.C., by Bishop Alexander M. Zaleski of Lansing, Michigan, as chairman of the Committee on Doctrine of the National Conference of Catholic Bishops. (This report was released in November 1969.)

Beginning in 1967, the so-called Pentecostal Movement has spread among the Catholic faithful. . . . It must be admitted that theologically the movement has legitimate reasons for existence. It has a strong biblical basis. It would be difficult to inhibit the working of the Spirit which manifested itself so abundantly in the early Church. The participants in the Catholic Pentecostal Movement claim that they receive certain charismatic gifts. Admittedly, there have been abuses, but the cure is not a denial of their existence but their proper use. . . . Perhaps our most prudent way to judge the validity of the claims of the Pentecostal Movement is to observe the effects on those who participate in the prayer meeting. There are many indications that this participation leads to a better understanding of the role the Christian plays in the Church. Many have experienced progress in their spiritual life. They are attracted to the reading of the Scriptures and a deeper understanding of their faith. They seem to grow in their attachment to certain established devotional patterns such as devotion to the Real Presence and the Rosary.

It is the conclusion to the Committee on Doctrine that the movement should, at this point, not be inhibited but allowed to develop. Certain cautions, however, must be expressed. Proper supervision can be effectively exercised only if the bishops keep in mind their pastoral responsibility to oversee and guide this movement in the Church. We must be on guard that they avoid the mistakes of classic Pentecostalism. It must be recognized that in our culture there is a tendency to substitute religious experience for religious doctrine. In practice, we recommend that bishops involve prudent priests to be associated with this movement. Such involvement and guidance would be welcome by the Catholic Pentecostals.

In 1968, it was estimated that 30,000 Roman Catholics had come into the baptism in the Holy Spirit. Although there are no accurate statistics available, recently a Jesuit Priest estimated that nearly one million Roman Catholics have now become involved in the Pentecostal movement.

The United Presbyterian Church in the United States of America, with concern for this movement of the Holy Spirit, also set up a committee to study the phenomena. After two years of thorough investigation and study, the committee reported to the 182nd General Assembly of their Church and published their findings in a 56-page booklet titled "The Work of the Holy Spirit." The following is excerpted from it:

... The movement was found to be dynamic, growing, and involving persons from practically every denomination, walk, and station in life. Varied educational backgrounds and personality patterns are present and the socioeconomic status ranges from the uneducated through those in high executive positions carrying great responsibility in major corporations, in federal government and in the space effort. Physicians, psychologists, psychiatrists, scientists, professor of every description, clergy of every denomination including the hierarchy, and professors of religion and philosophy are to be found in the movement. . . .
... We believe the church needs to pray for a sensitivity to see the manifestations of the Holy Spirit in our world today. We are not unmindful that the problems of discrimination between the true and fraudulent are considerable, but we must not allow the problems to paralyze our awareness to his presence, nor should we permit our fear of the unknown and the unfamiliar to close our minds against being surprised by grace. We know the misuse of mystical experience is an ever-present possibility, but that is no reason to preclude its appropriate use. We believe that those who are newly endowed with gifts and perceptions of the Spirit have an enthusiasm and joy to give and we also believe that those who rejoice in our traditions of having all things done in "decency and order" have a sobering depth to give. We therefore plead for a mutuality of respect and affection.

. . . The criteria by which we judge the validity of another's religious experience must ever be its compatibility with the mind and spirit of our Lord Jesus Christ, as we know them in the New Testament. If the consequence and quality of a reported encounter of the Holy Spirit be manifestly conducive to division, self-righteousness, hostility, exaggerated claims of knowledge and power, then the experience is subject to serious question. However, when the experience clearly results in new dimensions of faith, joy, and blessings to others, we must conclude that this is "what the Lord hath done" and offer him our praise.

In regard to the controversial issue of "speaking in tongues" they state:

. . . The practice of speaking in tongues, when inspired by the Holy Spirit, should not be over-emphasized; normally they belong to private worship. Christians who have experienced, through speaking in tongues, a revitalizing of their faith should be on guard against forming divisive cliques within the congregation. On the other hand, those who have received no unusual experiences of the Holy Spirit should be alert to the possibilities of a deeper understanding of the Gospel of Christ and a fuller participation in the gifts and fruit of the Spirit—of which love is the greatest. (I Cor. 13:13.)

As more and more people, both clergy and laity, come into this experience, they are turning to their respective denominations for guidance and support. I fail to see how any one denomination can adequately offer this guidance and support without first

45

having made an intensive study of all that is involved. It is my earnest prayer that many more studies will be made on the work of the Holy Spirit in the near future.

6. KNOW IT BEFORE
   YOU KNOCK IT

September 1968 found us entering into our usual fall schedule once again after a busy but relatively uneventful summer. Having by now adequately digested all the events of the previous spring, I knew the time had come to gradually begin sharing this new dimension of the Holy Spirit with my congregation. In preparing to do this, I found invaluable assistance from the booklet, *Receiving The Holy Spirit*, by the Rev. Robert Hall, Rector of the Church of The Holy Comforter, in Miami, Florida. He is an Episcopal priest who had come into this experience eight years previously. Also in preparation, I had bought 200 copies of *Good News For Modern Man*, a modern translation of the New Testament, and had placed them in every pew. Then, little by little in my Sunday morning sermons I began unfolding the story of my months of searching, always asking the congregation to read along in their individual Bibles each time I referred to an appropriate passage from scripture. Sunday after Sunday I reminded them, "Know it before you knock it! Until you have first investigated this seemingly new and unfamiliar approach for yourself as I have, you don't have the right to criticize it. Know it before you knock it!"

On the third Sunday in September we were privileged to have the Rev. Dennis Bennett as our guest preacher. As mentioned previously, he had been successfully preaching the baptism in the Holy Spirit in his church for 10 years. Very conveniently for us, he was in Pittsburgh to speak at the FGBMFI and kindly accepted our invitation to preach. Dennis is an extremely dynamic speaker and his sermon proved to be a most valuable addition to the groundwork I was by then laying.

October's sermons continued in much the same pattern, always firmly rooted in scripture. Then, on the third Sunday of that month, I finally explained to my people that Joanne and I had been baptized in the Holy Spirit and that both of us had received the gift of tongues, emphasizing that we were finding both gifts to be tremendous assets to our personal spiritual growth. In doing so, I caught Joanne more by surprise than anyone. All she could think of was, "Of all days to be exposed! Today's the church picnic and now that everyone knows, I'll either be avoided like the plague all afternoon or backed into a corner with questions." Neither was the case, however. Only one woman asked a question that afternoon and she was genuinely interested. No one else questioned anything and no one avoided us. The picnic turned out to be no different from any other. We drove home that evening bearing only the very justifiable criticism that both of us had cheated and used hard-boiled eggs in the egg toss contest.

The next Sunday I announced that a series of six

Bible studies on the Holy Spirit would begin that following Tuesday night. It was most encouraging to have over 60 men and women turn out for the first session. I began by teaching some of the scriptural references to the baptism in the Holy Spirit and then opened the meeting to discussion and sharing. After the first two sessions I realized that women were dominating the discussion. I spoke to some of them about my concern, and we all agreed to pray that more men would become involved so that no one would mistakenly view this baptism in the Holy Spirit as merely an emotional outlet for a few over-sensitive women.

Our prayers were quickly answered. That very next Sunday, after church, Jim greeted me rather surprisingly when he shook my hand.

"I think you've got me hooked," he said. I wasn't at all sure what he meant and there wasn't time for him to explain then, but less than an hour later he phoned me at home. This time he greeted me with joyful certainty.

"I *am* hooked," he said. "I know I've received the baptism in the Holy Spirit you've been preaching about. I received it while I was sitting there in church today listening to your sermon. It's hard to explain but something happened to me!"

That same Sunday evening, Tony, who had been attending our Tuesday night meetings, had gone to a Prayer and Praise meeting at Russ Bixler's church. At the appropriate time he said, "Would you pray for me to receive the baptism in the Holy Spirit?" That night his prayer was answered. The next day when I heard that Tony had been baptized in the

Spirit, I thanked the Lord. We had asked him for men and he had given us two in one day.

That next Tuesday evening started out just like the two preceding Tuesday evenings, but gradually the Spirit began to lead us out in a new direction. As usual, I stood in the pulpit and taught for awhile; then, people again volunteered stories of how Jesus had been especially alive to them in their life that past week. Next, I called upon Jim and Tony to share what had happened to them.

Jim, who works as an engineering analyst, told of his Sunday morning experience during the church service. He then began to analyze this experience with a scientific approach. I wasn't quite sure I followed all he said, but most of our men seemed to listen without apparent difficulty, and with obvious respect for what he was saying. Then Tony shared, telling of his search, his religious background and how he had found something which made Jesus so much more real to him.

They finished, and I talked for a few more minutes. I knew this was the night I was to step out in faith. The Spirit seemed to be saying to me, "Now is the time!" Somewhat boldly, I made an announcement.

"We have been talking about the baptism in the Holy Spirit for some time now," I started. "I'm sure many of you would like to receive this gift. We will end the meeting now. Those who want prayer for the baptism in the Holy Spirit will please come up to the choir stalls. Those who do not may leave the church quietly."

I didn't want to force anyone into the choir stalls

or prevent anyone from leaving if they desired. As a further opportunity for each one to choose, I said, "I'm going into the sacristy to put on my cassock. When I come out, we will begin praying for those who have come up to the choir stalls."

I went into the sacristy and began to put on my cassock. The thought went through my mind, "What if no one comes up?" But it was already much too late to think about that!

Then I opened the sacristy door and to my utter amazement, the choir stalls were filled with people! Still being very "green" concerning the best procedure to use, I took a folding chair and set it down near the center of the altar rail between two of the choir stalls. Beside me stood my good friend Milton whom I had avoided that previous winter because he was "to religious." I had asked him to pray with me when the people came forward.

I looked over to my right and sitting on the very end was "Doc." He was not an M.D. but a Ph.D., and at present was teaching at the University of Pittsburgh Medical School. I motioned for Doc to come forward. As he got up from the choir stall, the horrible thought went through my mind, "What if we pray for all these people and nothing happens to any of them?" But it was too late to think about that now, and I could only recall the words of our Lord, "Ask and it shall be given." Doc sat down in the chair and Milton and I laid hands on him in prayer. Within seconds Doc began to cry and it was beautiful ... he began to speak in tongues, and I prayed under my breath, "O Lord, we're in! Thank you, Jesus."

51

Doc got up. I looked to my left this time and motioned to another fellow, Bill, a research chemist, to come forward. Bill barely made it to the chair when, immediately, with great joy, he began to speak forth in a new language also. Our hands had hardly touched him, yet he, too, had been baptized in Jesus' Spirit. And so it went on that night. When we left the church around 20 additional people had come into this experience and almost all had received the gift of tongues. It had happened at St. Martin's—and a great many of those it had happened to were men!

During that week, my phone rang often with people asking questions and the curiosity grew. The next Tuesday evening found us again at the church, with much expectancy and enthusiasm. However, everything went decently and in order. There was no shouting; no swinging from the chandeliers; no rolling in the aisles. Just prayer, scripture reading, praising God and many more shared experiences.

Once again it came time for prayers for the baptism in the Holy Spirit. I, too, was continuing to grow. I had asked myself, "Why a chair for people to sit in to receive this baptism in the Holy Spirit?" We in the church are accustomed to kneeling for prayer and praying at the altar rail, so let's kneel at the altar rail. After all, Jesus is the baptizer and there is no set physical form or procedure mentioned in scripture as to how to receive. I informed the people of my intention, commenting that we were just children of God with sincerity of heart, wanting more of Jesus and His Holy Spirit. The Lord honored our request and a dozen more received the blessing.

We were about the leave the church, and I had just turned out the lights at the altar, when one of our men, another Jim, a computer engineer, walked in the door and hurriedly came up to me.

"George," he said, "I had to come back. I was all the way home, but I had to come back. Please pray for me to receive the baptism in the Holy Spirit."

"Sure," I replied, and I motioned to a few of my people to go forward with us to the altar rail. I was about to talk to Jim about salvation and forgiveness of sins, but before I could complete one sentence, he interrupted loudly.

"I have to say something—Jesus Christ, I accept you as my Lord and Saviour," and immediately he burst forth in tongues.

Our group on Tuesday began to attract more and more people of all denominations. People came from all over the city. Some were merely curious, to be sure, but most of them came with a sincere desire for more of the Lord. By the fall of 1970, we were averaging as many as 150 people per night at these meetings and they began to lose some of their original informality. So we chose to add a Saturday night meeting as well. Although the majority of those coming now have already received salvation and the baptism in the Holy Spirit, a few new people still come into these experiences after almost every meeting.

For most of us who decided to know it, then found we couldn't knock it, the baptism in the Holy

Spirit has become normal, routine procedure and we have settled down to the much more demanding business of walking daily in the Spirit.

7. THEY'LL NEVER DRIVE ME OUT OF THIS CHURCH!!

Then there's Frank. Frank came to St. Martin's 12 years ago from Buffalo with his lovely wife, Nancy, and their two daughters. Frank had been raised in the Russian Orthodox Church, and took his religion quite seriously. Although their spiritual life had begun to wane somewhat while in Buffalo, he and Nancy, who had been a Lutheran before their marriage, came looking for a church home when they moved to Monroeville. They wanted something which would make them both feel comfortable in worshipping the Lord. Besides that, their daughters were now in their formative years and they wanted them brought up in the atmosphere of the church. After visiting St. Martin's, they decided to make it their spiritual home. This proved to be much to our advantage.

Frank became very active in the church—both in his time given to its operation and spiritually. He was always ready to serve in any capacity when needed.

When the time arrived for the "big push"—that is,

the final campaign drive to build the church proper and additional church school rooms and offices—I approached Frank to be my building fund chairman and he accepted. Frank had many assets to offer: sincerity, dedication and a good mind. As a scientist he already had over 150 patents in his name. He also had a great desire to see the final church built. During the actual campaign drive, Frank and I became very close. One November he spoke at "cottage meetings," attended by small groups of our people. For 11 straight nights, he talked about St. Martin's and our plans.

The campaign was a success and the church was built. I recall writing Frank a letter in which I thanked him for so much time and devotion and also expressing my opinion that he was truly "on fire with the Holy Spirit!" In the days that followed, Frank was elected to the vestry, and I considered it a privilege to appoint him as my senior warden.

After serving his three-year term on the vestry, Frank felt it only right to have other men serve in that capacity in order that they might better understand, first-hand, the workings of the church. He concentrated now on being a layreader and actively participating in the Brotherhood of St. Andrew. Then, too, his secular job began to require more of his time during the week and he was travelling more for his company.

It was only a few months later that we began to move into this new dimension of the work of the Holy Spirit. Frank's work kept him away from many of the early discussions, but when he did hear of many of our women going to prayer meetings and healing services across town, he began to simply ask me over and over again, "Why can't the same thing happen right here in our own church? We believe the Holy Spirit is in every church, so why isn't He more active here?" I told Frank the Spirit was active here and that we were seeing more and more activity at our church. Frank began to attend the meetings again, but by this time was becoming confused. He began to resist what I was teaching and preaching.

The crowning blow came when, innocently but very unwisely, a member of the church went up to Frank after one Prayer and Praise meeting and said, "Don't worry, Frank. We're praying for you and in time you'll get the Holy Spirit, too!!" This was typical of some of the unfortunate comments that others made to him in the following weeks. Although they were spoken in sincerity, he found each one more provoking than the last, and finally stopped attending the Prayer and Praise meetings altogether.

Over the next few months, I found it increasingly difficult to communicate with Frank. As more of our people received the baptism in the Holy Spirit, he became even more defensive in his views, especially when those whom he knew quite well would receive this gift.

It was during this period that Frank could be heard proclaiming: "No one will drive me out of this church!" Of course, the feeling that anyone was trying to drive him out of the church was clearly a false assumption, but the more he was approached the more upset he became. The feeling of irritation on his part was quite natural, and, of course, the chances of his becoming more open to the possibilities of this new movement were greatly lessened because of all these untimely, unfortunate episodes.

Very shortly after this, I began my adult confirmation classes. These were opened to include any who desired to come and take a refresher course in the life of the Church. Since we had a youth workshop on Sunday evenings for grades four through six and our junior and senior high youth met as well at that time, many parents would attend the presentations in order to learn a little more while waiting for their children. Of course, the main purpose of the classes was to instruct those adults who were to be confirmed by the Bishop later that year.

This year, besides talking about the normal approach to receiving God's Holy Spirit at Confirmation, I also talked about this new outpouring of the Holy Spirit, quoting Acts 2 and I Corinthians 12. I began to tell of the experiences of people in our church as well as in other denominations and throughout the world.

Frank was somewhat irritated by my words when I said it was possible to receive "a large chunk or an abundance of the Holy Spirit" at one time, instead of just a little bit of the Spirit at a time. I talked about Pentecost and the gifts of the Holy Spirit. Frank became even more defensive.

"I'll grow gracefully," he remarked, "the way the Prayerbook says by daily increasing in the Holy Spirit—that's for me!"

The meeting ended on that note, abrupt as it was. As he was about to leave, I called him aside.

"Frank," I said. "I'm going to be out of town next

Sunday night. How about you leading the discussion for the class?"

He was flabbergasted. "You know my feelings."

"Yes," I said, "but I trust you. I've told them my views. Now you can tell them yours."

The following Sunday evening he did take the classes, and he did express his views, and thereafter he seemed much more willing to listen to views other than his own. Becoming curious once again, a month later when we had our teaching mission on the Holy Spirit, led by the Rev. Dennis Bennett, he appeared at the very first meeting on Sunday evening. He was back for the Monday evening session, and after it ended he went home. As he said later, all night long he "tossed and turned" in bed. Tuesday took him to New York for his company and, as Frank says, "The strangest thing happened. The meeting I attended ended early and by sheer luck I was able to get a reservation back to Pittsburgh on an early flight." When the meeting began, he was in his pew listening intently. When the meeting ended, he was at the altar rail receiving the baptism in the Holy Spirit! His older daughter, Karen, also came into the experience that night. Nancy had come into the experience a few months earlier. Not long after, Carol, his other daughter, received as well. No one has driven Frank out of his church. He and his family are now more a part of St. Martin's than ever.

A few other active, dedicated people in the parish also misinterpreted some of my teaching at first and became irritated, as Frank had. Two such people were Charlie and his wife, Lavonna. Charlie owns and operates his own plumbing and heating business. When we began holding our first Prayer and Praise meetings, they had been members of St. Martin's for nine years. They did not attend the first six weeks of meetings and when they did come for the first time, they rebelled afterward.

"We have the Holy Spirit," he said indignantly. "How can anyone tell us we need the Holy Spirit?"

"Of course, they had the Holy Spirit. They loved God, too, and they were constantly serving Him in the church. Together they had sponsored our youth group for five years. Charlie had also been Men's Club president, vestryman, junior warden, and senior warden. Lavonna was just as reliable and tireless in her work with the women, especially in the kitchen. Whatever the occasion—bazaars, luncheons, dinners, wedding receptions—they were on the scene in one capacity or another, most often working as a team.

Once they realized that, while they did certainly have the Holy Spirit, they could have still more of His presence in their lives through this baptism in the Holy Spirit, they too received. Charlie and Lavonna continue to be reliable, seemingly tireless servants in all their former capacities, but now they are balancing those efforts with their equally enthusiastic efforts in the spiritual realm. They have become avid, daily students of the Bible. Lavonna leads the singing at both the Tuesday and Saturday night meetings. Charlie, since receiving his baptism in the Holy Spirit, has become an accomplished speaker and loves any opportunity to share how much Jesus means to him. In their spiritual work, too, he and Lavonna most often work together as a team. More and more, they are being called to share their love and enthusiasm for the Lord with churches all over the city and sometimes out of the state as well.

Irritation is very much a part of Mary's story, too, although the reason for it differs from the others. She and her family have been very active in the parish since they came to us over 11 years ago. She has a beautiful, well-trained soprano voice and sang in our choir until 1961 when she developed a throat condition which necessitated her resigning. Her doctor explained that if she didn't stop singing she would soon lose her voice entirely. He advised her not to even speak any more than absolutely necessary, especially in crowds where she would have to speak with more volume. The condition did not improve. She was almost continually hoarse, many times losing her voice altogether.

Singing had always been very much a part of Mary's life so that, having to live year after year with this condition and its imposed restrictions, she grew more and more discouraged and resentful. She often sat in tears as she listened to the choir's anthem and was constantly annoyed by well-meaning friends who would inquire as to whether or not her condition was improving.

One Wednesday morning, two years ago, she arrived a little late for the regular meeting of our women's prayer group. She had always been a regular member of the group and a most valuable asset, but that morning as she sat down among them, they were singing and she suddenly resented them bitterly. She now began to look on these, some of her best-loved friends, as just a "bunch of pious people."

As the women stopped singing and went on into prayer, she herself prayed.

"Lord, take these negative feelings from me. I know I can't be used when I feel like this."

By the time the meeting was over, Mary's bitter resentment had been replaced with love and she went on into the church with the others for the Communion and Healing Service. At the end of the service, after everyone had the laying on of hands, I offered the final prayer and then, turning around, saw Mary still kneeling alone at the altar rail. I went over and asked if she was all right.

"Yes," she said, "but I really want this."

"Really want what, Mary?"

"This baptism."

I prayed for her right then and she immediately received.

The next afternoon she was vacuuming her living room and, without realizing at first what she was doing, she began to sing one of the musical scales and then another and still another. Then she sang scores from several different arias. Her voice was back! After eight long years of silence, she was singing again! She immediately phoned several different women from the prayer group and sang for them over the phone. When her three children arrived home from school, she greeted them eagerly.

"Guess what? God gave me back my voice!"

We all rejoiced with her. In receiving this gift of the baptism in the Holy Spirit, she had received a gift of healing as well.

Mary still has to be careful not to abuse her voice, but she has now returned to the choir and sings with them every other Sunday. On those "other" Sundays she teaches the seventh grade Sunday School class. That requires a voice, too. She has her voice back again and is using it to the glory of God.

Irritation was very much a part of Alan's story, too. I'll let him tell you how in his own words.

"Last Palm Sunday (my first real one) will always be very special to me. As I stood in church, giving my personal testimony for Jesus Christ before several hundred fellow Episcopalians, I saw faces reflecting understanding, hope, love, embarrassment, and downright cold disgust. Let me go back and tell you some of the circumstances that led to my being there in that unique position.

"Though my wife and I were Protestants when we decided to get married, we lacked a common denominational point of contact, so we decided to compromise and chose my wife's aunt's church, St. Paul's Episcopal. Eventually we were confirmed and became properly staid, complacent, secure-in-the-Prayerbook-Episcopalians. Sporadic church attendance, along with getting our girls to church school, became our norm . . . just spare us any church activity.

"About a year prior to that Palm Sunday, I had transferred from Colorado and, since we settled in Monroeville, St. Martin's was our logical choice for a church. Immediately, I noticed a new and different atmosphere. There were some scattered and sincere "Good mornings" and the first Sunday Bill even said, "If you like to sing, come join the choir." The real stopper was that our rector, Father Stockhowe, preached joy, happiness, and Christian love and other near-heretical messages, right there in public. Like any decent (believing?) Christian, I knew that our faith was based on sorrow, heaviness of spirit, and a true, dogmatic and ritualistic propriety, so his sermons became increasingly upsetting.

"Finally, just a month or so before this great Sunday, I told my wife that as soon as our youngest was confirmed (which was to be very shortly), I didn't think I'd ever go to church again. Although Father Stockhowe had been preaching a live Jesus and the need to accept Him as the basis of true faith, Luke 4 reminds us that a prophet is not recognized in his own land. So I did not become electrified until another one of our own genuine Episcopalian evangelists, Father Dennis Bennett, came preaching the same message. He said Jesus was alive; that He wanted to come into our hearts; and that there was an eternal, joyous life ahead. This promise was so compelling that my wife, seated beside me, sensed an instant change in me. After hearing his brief sermon and his first evening's address, I was unable to attend any more of these sessions, but the Word of God was implanted, and man! did it grow?! The following weekend, Father Stockhowe gave me two or three helpful explanatory booklets on salvation and the baptism in the Holy Spirit.

"The very next night, alone in a motel room in Huntingdon, Pennsylvania, with a loud drinking party going on across the hall, I knelt by the bed. After confessing every sin I could think of, I told Jesus how much I loved Him, that I couldn't go on without Him, and that I wanted Him to come into my heart and take over my life. Instantly, He did! A flowing warmth descended over me and in that moment I experienced 'the peace that passeth all understanding.' Years of error and sin lifted as He took my burden. Right then, in my exuberance, I asked Jesus to baptize me in the Holy Spirit and He granted me this additional blessing of added strength for my new life in Christ.

"You may ask how long this experience lasted. Well, it started a year ago this weekend and 'is still doing nicely.' Does this mean that I was perfect overnight? No, and I never will be in this life; hence, my joy in having Jesus Christ as my Saviour. Every day I find new areas of my life that need cleansing, repairing, and strengthening. Several months after this experience of salvation and my personal Pentecost, I started to write a protest poem about churches always being locked. After I was well into the poem, the Holy Spirit took over and showed me where the locks really are. I'm sure you can tell where the Holy Spirit took over and helped me finish the poem in a most positive manner and in record time. You who may read and then wonder, don't miss this free and wonderful gift of salvation."

LOCKED

I travelled to a church one day
To spend a quiet time in prayer
And the hope and joy that filled me
Made me glad that I was there.
But my heart was quickly saddened
And my mind and soul were shocked
As I pulled back on the handle
And found the door was locked.

I stood there in dismay awhile
And slowly then I turned away.
I said I'd find another church.
I'd try again, some other day.
So through the years from town to town
I'd try one where I'd not be mocked.
But every time I'd try the door
I'd always find that it was locked.

So I quit trying after while
And thought I'd leave my life to fate.
Then one day God made known to me
"My son, don't be impatient . . . wait!"
Well, I relaxed a little bit and
Finally, when completely calm,
God made me open up His Book
And read the Thirty-second Psalm.

I really took God at His word
And many were the ones I told
But as time passed and no word came
My cherished hope again grew cold.
And Satan perched upon my brow
He lied and finally let me see
That God's so busy everywhere,
He really hadn't time for me.

Well, I believed him, like the rest,
And weighted down I trudged the road
Until a stranger passed one day
And called out, "Why the heavy load?"
"I tried to ask the Lord for help,
But the way in every case was blocked,
And every time I've tried a church
The outer door was always locked."

His laughter filled the afternoon
And though annoyed, I stopped awhile
And waited 'til he'd settled down.
His face glowed with the warmest smile.
He said God's door is never closed.
Now this news gave me quite a start
But he said that the only lock
Was right there on my human heart.

Well, I looked in upon that heart
As we stood talking in the dust
And saw that he had told the truth
Both hinge and hasp were solid rust.
I don't know where the stranger went
But I trudged down the road some more
Intent on how to open up
That solid, useless, rusty door.

I heaved and heaved and heaved again
And with a crash it opened wide.
A flood of joy swept over me
For Jesus Christ was just outside.
I knelt and cried, "Am I too late?"
He only smiled and entered in
And stretching forth His mighty arm,
He snatched away my load of sin.

He said, "I've been here many times
But every time I paused and knocked
I turned away most sorrowfully
In finding that this door was locked."
He said, "My arms are open wide;
No one has reason to be late
Until the tolling of the bell
Says death has closed the final gate."

My days have never been the same
Since Jesus came to stay with me;
And He is laying out His plans
And telling what's in store, you see?
Now sometimes I have slipped a bit.
I've gotten creased and slightly soiled.
But every day I use that door
And always keep those hinges oiled.

My friend, please open up your heart
And let Christ's breath of life sweep in.
Get rid of all your earthly cares.
Let Jesus take your load of sin.
Take time to counsel if you will
The lame, the ill or just those bored.
Just let them know the wonderment
And promise of our Risen Lord.
While some will joyously believe,
Still some will sneer or just be shocked.
But tell them all it's not too late
And Jesus' door is never locked.

Of course, St. Martin's doors always have been
and always will be open to everyone. I cannot emphasize that enough! It is my sincere prayer that no
one will ever be driven out of our congregation or be
discouraged from choosing us as their church family.
I pray that no one, upon reading this book, will get
the erroneous impression that we are interested only
in those people who are interested in the baptism in
the Holy Spirit. We always have and always will ex-
tend our warmest welcome to everyone regardless of
where they are or where they choose to be in their
personal spiritual walk.

At Christ Episcopal Church, North Hills, I discovered the following prayer in their informational brochure. It is their prayer for Christ Church, North Hills. It is also my prayer for St. Martin's, Monroeville:

Oh God our Heavenly Father, make the door of our Parish Church wide enough to receive all who need human love and fellowship and a Father's care; and narrow enough to shut out all envy, pride and uncharitableness. Make its threshold smooth enough to be no stumbling-block to children, to weak or straying feet; but rugged and strong enough to turn back the tempter's power. O Heavenly Father, make the door to our Parish Church a gateway to Thy eternal Kingdom. Bless every member and worker in our Parish. May all that we do be to Thy Honor and Glory, the upbuilding of our Parish, and the extension of Thy Kingdom. May we continue to be Thine forever and daily increase in Thy Holy Spirit of love and service to others; through Jesus Christ our Lord and Saviour. Amen.

8. THE GIFTS FOR
THE GREEKS

In Matthew 7:8 we read, "For everyone who asks will receive" and our friends who came to us from the Greek Orthodox faith were certainly no exception.

One of the first Greeks to appear at one of our Prayer and Praise meetings was Georgia, a very attractive woman in her early 20s. Georgia had been searching for something to fill the void in her life. She had been reading and investigating astrology, meditation and other psychic phenomena.

That first Tuesday evening was not her last. She returned again and again, finally asking for and receiving the baptism. Not long after, she brought her brother, Nick, and he, too, became a frequent visitor on Tuesday evenings. Before long their mother, Grace, was with them. Grace also became intrigued. She told other relatives about our meetings and they also began to come. Among them were a few college students, one of whom was Tina, a freshman at California State Teachers College.

On the night that she received, Tina returned home to share her experience with her mother Mary, who had not yet been to St. Martin's.

70

"Let me read to you from the Bible, Mother," she said. "It's so beautiful."

At first her mother was not too impressed, but Tina, in her newly-found joy, went on. "Mother, will you pray with me and if I pray in tongues will you laugh?"

"No, Tina, I won't laugh. Go ahead and pray."

They sat down on the stairs. Tina began to pray in her new tongue and then began to cry. Her mother relates it this way:

"It was so wonderful. She was crying and I began to cry. Then I began to get a feeling in my body—a sensation like electricity. I told Tina, 'something from you has come into me.' "

Mary had received the baptism in the Holy Spirit sitting right there on the stairs of her own home. She began to share her experience with others of her faith and they all began to realize that they didn't have to come to St. Martin's to receive. It could happen to anybody, anywhere.

More and more of the Greeks came into the experience and many of them began to share their newly-found joy and love with their priests and bishops. Since so many of their people had been going to St. Martin's with such apparent regularity, their clergy began to wonder if they were seeking another religion or something contrary to Orthodox doctrine. Then, too, they thought perhaps St. Martin's might be trying to "steal their people."

Accordingly, Georgia's mother, Grace, who had also come into the experience by this time, decided to invite some of our St. Martin's people and me, along with some of her Greek friends, to a Prayer

71

and Praise meeting in her home one Saturday evening. She also invited her former priest who was now a bishop. He came and brought with him the dean of their local cathedral. We all sang and prayed together and then began to share.

One of the Orthodox laymen told of how the Liturgy on Sunday mornings, as he put it, "always seemed dead." But now so much of it had come alive for him, and he could appreciate it so much more. Many of the group expressed similar feelings. I then spoke of my great desire to preach this experience of the baptism to everyone and also of my desire that people remain faithful to their respective churches upon receiving so that they might be more effective witnesses of God's abundant love.

As the evening came to an end, one of the Greeks asked the Bishop what he thought of this new approach and he replied, "If it brings you closer to God and people and makes you love them more, then it's of the Lord and it's good. I see nothing wrong with your continuing."

Shortly after this, the Bishop and many of us left for home; but some of the Greeks stayed behind and ministered to one another in prayer. When they concluded that night, a few more received this baptism, one of whom was Toula's husband.

The next morning, Toula and her friend, Ann, talked on the phone for well over an hour and a half. Ann knew the Lord was using her in that conversation. As they discussed more and more about the baptism, Toula became irritated.

"I'm good," she said dogmatically. "I'm happy. I don't need anything else." But they continued and then as Toula later expressed it, "I began to feel goose pimples and a warmth within me."

Ann went on, "You know, Toula, it's really easy to receive this gift from God. If you are really sincere, ask Jesus to forgive you of your sins. Ask Him to give you the gift of the Holy Spirit, to baptize you with the Holy Spirit, and then just thank Him. That's what we do with Father Stockhowe at St. Martin's."

With that their conversation ended and they hung up. But the warmth and goose pimples that Toula had felt did not subside. She began to pray.

"Jesus, forgive me for my sins. And Jesus, please give me the gift of Your Holy Spirit." At that moment, she felt an intense warmth all over, as she tells it, "from the top of my head to the tip of my toes." It grew to even greater intensity than before. She knew it was God's presence. Her feeling of joy was overwhelming, but as yet she had not spoken in tongues. Everything was so wonderful that she found herself saying over and over again, "Thank you, thank you, thank you." The Spirit was overflowing. She just couldn't say thank you enough. Then she began to say thank you over and over again in Greek, whereupon she went on to speak neither English nor Greek, but words she had never spoken before. The Lord had given her a new tongue—a new language in which to praise Him!

Ann continued to be used by the Lord. When Holy Week arrived, she found herself at church more than ever before. She attended every service that week. At home, she spent much more time in prayer than she did in preparing the traditional

Easter foods. At the Holy Thursday service, she and all the others in attendance were aware that their priest, Father Constantine, was losing his voice. He could barely be heard during the service. Following the service, he explained to them that he had been to his doctor that afternoon concerning his voice and that the doctor had advised him not to speak. "But," Father added, "how can I do that this time of year?" Ann, along with Mary, Toula, and several others went back into the sanctuary and prayed for the healing of their priest's throat. The next day, as he began the Good Friday service, it was very apparent that his voice had returned to normal.

Carol, a young housewife, also came into the experience of this baptism in the Holy Spirit, as did her husband. They had always been active in the church and served it well, but now they were more enthusiastic than ever. They, along with many of their friends, began to think of the next step.

"How are we going to get a Prayer and Praise meeting started in our church?"

"Be open and honest," I advised them. "Go tell your priest about your personal experience and ask him what you should do about it."

Although many had spoken briefly to him about what had happened to them, none had actually told him their complete story. Carol felt led to do so and met with him in his study soon after that.

"The baptism in the Holy Spirit is so beautiful," she said. Now I know Jesus is right here next to me all the time and I can communicate with Him so much better."

"Well, that's what's wrong with Protestant theology," her priest replied. "They have all those songs about walking and talking with Jesus, but you just can't do that really. He's a Godhead. He's almighty. He's awesome. You can't walk and talk with Him personally."

"Have I done anything against Orthodoxy?" she asked. "I don't think I have, but I want to know what you think."

He assured her she had done nothing wrong, that the experience of speaking in tongues was entirely scriptural and in Greek was called glossolalia. He told her that her experience was legitimate but that he did not think it was necessary for everyone to have it.

She then explained about the third annual conference on the Holy Spirit to be held that next week in Pittsburgh and asked him to attend and then express his views on it. He agreed to do so. They ended with prayer and Carol left.

The next week, Father Constantine did go to some of the conference sessions with his people. Later, at his teachers' meeting and Bible study at the Church that same week, he shared some of his observations. As his parishioners put it, "That night Father seemed to have a special radiance as he so freely read the Bible and talked about the conference. He was especially gratified to hear so much emphasis being placed on the sacrament of Holy Communion at the conference. He commented, 'Now I realize more than ever that Orthodoxy does have something tremendous to share. We should start opening our doors to Christians of all denominations.'"

When the meeting was over, he called Carol aside

and said, "You know, Carol, I think we should begin holding Prayer and Praise meetings." Carol's prayers had been answered. They held their first meeting the following Monday. Only six people attended. One week later there were 17. At last count, there were over 40.

My story of the Greeks would not be complete without telling you about Gus. He has been a member of the Merchant Marine almost all of his life. In Gus's words:

"I've been a Christian all of my life, but I had read some books while sailing about the life of Jesus which made me doubt Him. One day, while at sea, I felt like praying and I began to pray every morning and evening. Not long after this, the tone of my wife's letters began to change. She was talking more and more about religion, about Jesus. She kept talking about the Holy Spirit and about going to St. Martin's. Every letter was more and more about religion, so I said to her in my letters, 'How about writing about something else besides religion?' "

Last April his wife, Ann, went to Jacksonville to meet him in port there for a few days. As they walked together along the beach one morning, she asked him if he would like to receive the baptism in the Holy Spirit, too.

"Yes," he responded, "but you'll have to pray. I don't think I can pray."

She did pray with him that he would receive this gift, too. When they finished praying, a rainbow appeared in the clouds above their heads. They both saw it. As Gus now relates, "It was a different rainbow, though; only about 15 or 20 feet long. There was no rain, only clouds. It wasn't the kind of weather for rainbows, but we both saw one."

As he shared this experience with me, I could not help thinking of another seaman and another rainbow.

I do set my bow in the clouds, and it shall be a token of a covenant between me and the earth. And it shall come to pass when I bring a cloud over the earth, that the bow shall be seen in the cloud.

Genesis 9:13–14

God spoke these words to Noah. How beautifully appropriate that God had chosen to give Gus that same sign He had given to Noah, "a bow," as a sign that he had heard the prayer of his heart.

Gus did receive the baptism in the Holy Spirit that day. As he now tells it, "All I felt was love, just love. I just felt exhilarated, kind of like you get from alcohol, but this wasn't from alcohol."

Isn't that what Paul referred to when he told the Ephesians, "Be ye not drunk with wine, in which is excess, but be filled with the Spirit"? (Ephesians 5:18)

Gus is home on leave now—a new man; and you can be sure that when he goes off to sea once again, he'll be taking the good news of the Gospel all over the world with him. Now, as with so many of his fellow Greek friends and relatives, Jesus is more alive for him, too.

Now that the Greeks have their own thing going, we seldom see them any more. Father Constantine leads their Prayer and Praise meetings on Monday nights in the sanctuary of their beautiful new $800,-000 church. Just last month they invited me over to speak. The meeting was wonderful. They sang songs of praise, prayed, sang in tongues, and the gifts of prophecy and interpretation of tongues were in operation as well. After I had spoken, we concluded with prayer and went downstairs for coffee and cookies. Unknown to me, Mary, who refers to herself as "the bold one" asked only two people if they wanted to return upstairs for prayer. But then the word spread among the 70-some people who were there that night, and she found herself leading a procession back up to the sanctuary. I was encouraged to go by the sanctuary on my way out. There were the Greeks, up near the front of the church, ministering to one another and praying and singing in the Spirit. I waved farewell and headed home. It was thrilling to learn later that 12 more Greeks received the baptism in the Holy Spirit that night. New life and power continues to fall upon the Greek Orthodox as God continues to "pour out his Spirit."

Upon finishing this chapter about our Greek Orthodox friends, I took a copy over to Father Constantine to get his personal approval of all this information I had written about him and his people. After reading through it with me, he offered only one criticism:

"Why do you stop there? So much more has happened than that. You wrote nothing of all the healings we've recently had; how so many more people come to receive Holy Communion; or how our offerings have increased!"

"Wait a minute!" I interrupted. "If you want to tell about all that, you'll have to write your own book!" He just laughed and replied, "Give me another year and I will!"

9. IT HITS HOME

Lutheran pastor Larry Christenson, in his book *The Christian Family*, which I consider to be a classic in its field, refers to his own immediate family as a "Jesus family." While we haven't even come close to measuring up to all the ideals he presents for living together as a Jesus family, we are trying. As we look back over these past three years, we can see definite evidence that gradually we are all learning to let Jesus assume His rightful position as head of our household.

We have been blessed with three healthy sons—Mark, 13; George III, 11; and Christopher, 6. For them too Jesus is becoming more alive every day.

Mark received the baptism in the Holy Spirit in the spring of 1970 quite by his own choice. Prior to that time, he had heard and overheard the numerous conversations on the entire subject between Joanne and me. In addition, he is an avid reader, so it was not surprising to see him taking on *The Cross and the Switchblade*, and *They Speak with Other Tongues* among other books which we were now bringing into the house. We, ourselves, made no attempt to encourage him. I have heard of many children much younger than 12 receiving, but I feel that unless a child has reached the age of discretion before he receives, he will not be able to adequately understand and use the experience meaningfully. I feel it is up to Christian parents to decide when a child has reached the proper age. My earnest prayer is that this experience will never be looked upon by any parent as a substitute for his daily spiritual responsibility to the child involved.

In March 1970, the Rev. Dennis Bennett and his wife, Rita, returned to St. Martin's, this time for a three-day teaching mission on the Holy Spirit. While Dennis addressed the adults in the church the first evening, Rita addressed over 100 young people of all denominations in the parish hall. At the end of her simple, but beautiful witness she asked all those who wanted to know more about salvation or the baptism in the Holy Spirit to follow her over to the church library. Joanne was there in the parish hall taping Rita's presentation and was surprised to see Mark get up from a most sought-after position between his two favorite girls and follow Rita to the library. That's conviction!

By this time, Dennis had finished in the church and the adults mingled in the outside hall. Joanne and several other parents stood near the library waiting to take home their children, who had now been with Rita about 20 minutes. Soon the library door opened and out they came, one by one, looking for some parent or good friend to throw their arms around in joy. And then came Mark, beaming as Joanne had never seen him beam before. As he threw both his arms around her and hugged her, he could only say, "Mother" and she knew at once that he, too, had received the baptism in the Holy Spirit. The hall was now humming with excited conversations as the children tried to share the joy of their new gift with their parents, some of whom had not yet received it themselves. In the midst of all this, and often engaged in several different conversations at one time, Joanne lost Mark. It was almost 11 o'clock so she got her coat but still was unable to find him.

Then, someone pointed through the glass doors into the church, and there stood Mark in front of the choir stalls praying with two other boys who knelt below him in the front row. Having freely been given, he was already freely giving. It was then after 11 o'clock and a school day coming up, but Joanne could only think of Jesus' words to His mother when she found Him in the Temple at the age of 12, "Know ye not that I must be about my Father's business?" and she decided to wait a while longer.

In the year that has passed since that night, we have seen no dramatic change in Mark's life, but we have often gone into his bedroom and we are pleased to find his Bible lying open amidst all his science and space books and computer manuals. Mark has now added Jesus to his list of avid interests. We continue to pray that he will not only keep Him on his list but that he will keep Him on top.

Then there's George: "My-room's-always-spotless-but-don't-look-in-my-cupboard George." Only turning 11 now, we have no desire to encourage him to receive this baptism in the Holy Spirit, but he is growing spiritually in many beautiful ways. He loves to attend Saturday night Prayer and Praise meetings. Much of what goes on must be over his head and the meetings sometimes last over two hours, but back he goes, week after week, for more. During these past Christmas holidays, he had gone with Joanne to one of our Tuesday night Prayer and Praise meetings since he didn't have to get up for school the next morning. When the meeting was over and almost everyone had gone, about six of us stood talking in the hall. It was then that Norma noticed she had lost her car keys, so we all began to search the surrounding floor and stairs. Norma kept repeating, "I had them in my hand. Where could they be but on the floor here somewhere?" Joanne left the search early and began writing a note to the sexton, "Dear Ruth, If you find ..." but before she could finish the note Norma had found her keys with the help of young George. Unknown to any of us he had slipped into the church and prayed, "Dear Jesus, help us to find those car keys." Thereupon he left the church and walking over to Norma said, "Could it be in your boot?" referring to the low shoe-boots she was wearing. By now Norma was open to any suggestion, so she pulled off her right boot and out fell the car keys!

As young George later related on the way home, "I couldn't believe my eyes when I saw those car keys fall out of that boot," and neither could the rest of us. While all the others were taking the situation in their own hands, George had the wisdom to put it in the hands of the Lord. Why not? Isn't the same Lord who knows the very thoughts of our hearts also capable of knowing the whereabouts of our car keys? George thought he was. He kept saying, "Boy!

I don't know what ever made me think they were in her boot. It had to be Jesus who helped me think of that!" Once home, we used his experience in trying to explain the spiritual gifts of wisdom and knowledge to him. But through his simple faith, he had already taught us more than we could teach him that night.

As for Christopher, his, too, is a very simple but nonetheless profound faith. Spiritually it seems he, also, is sometimes teaching us much more than we have been able to teach him. With his prayers, as in almost everything else he does "No time like the present" is always his attitude. Our driveway at the rectory is rather steep and after a heavy snow we usually have to make several unsuccessful attempts to get the car up and out onto the front street. Christ is familiar with the situation and knows how impatient we both get when that happens. One snowy morning Joanne put Chris in the back of the car and then backed out of the garage. We had just had about four inches of new snow, but Joanne drove straight up the driveway without any trouble. As she drove on out onto the street, she heard a very brief, but enthusiastic, prayer being offered from the back seat, "Up on the first time! Thank you, Jesus!"

Joanne was bathing him one evening and, looking at two large ugly warts on the sole of his left foot, said to him:

"You remind me to call the doctor so we can go see him about those. I keep forgetting and I think they're getting bigger."

"Let's ask Jesus to make them go away," he replied. "Then we won't have to go to the doctor."

"Dear Jesus," he prayed right there in the bathtub, "make my warts go away. Thank you, Jesus."

Less than a week later we were amazed to find no sign of the warts or any indication that they had ever been there in the first place. But Chris knew they had been there, and he knew his Jesus had taken them away. Is it any wonder then that when his great grandfather died that fall he reacted:

"Great Grandpap's so lucky. He gets to see Jesus before we do."

Chris has a guitar and of all the different songs he sings his very favorite is "Stand Up and Shout If You Love My Jesus!" Every time we hear him sing it, we want to.

Our new life in the Spirit has brought Joanne and me much closer together as husband and wife. We can see that, as we're growing closer to Jesus, we're growing closer to each other as well. There had been numerous occasions in our first 11 years of married life when our quick tempers got the best of us and we would let the resulting anger run its destructive course. But that's not Christian marriage as it should be. We always knew it wasn't, but only in these past three years have we made an all-out attempt to do something about it.

I can't remember the last time we went through the long, silent treatment routine, but we still let our anger cloud the scene now and then. Last October, I returned home one afternoon about five o'clock from a wearisome day that had taken me all over the city to two different meetings and various hospital calls. Driving up our street, I was first irritated to see our boys and their friends riding bicycles over our front lawn. Walking in through our front hall, I found the television blaring in the living room with no one watching it and then, sitting down to read the paper in the family room, I discovered half of it was missing. Furthermore, instead of being in the kitchen getting dinner, Joanne was upstairs on a ladder painting Mark's bedroom. I asked myself why I had bothered to come home, and, after seeing the mood I was in, Joanne was wishing I hadn't. She too, was tired and the childish picking began.

"Where were you when the kids were riding on the lawn? Couldn't you hear TV blaring in the living room? What happened to the rest of the paper and when are we going to eat?"

To which Joanne, also weary from painting all day, made some very unlady-like replies. This established a miserable atmosphere which prevailed through dinner. As Joanne started the dishes, I reminded her very curtly that she had agreed to give some short instruction at the Prayer and Praise meeting that night and then I went out to play football with our boys. In her anger and despair, she sat down at the kitchen table and, while leafing through a copy of *Good News for Modern Man*, she began to pray.

"O, Father, help. We've done it again. I'm mad at him and he's mad at me. May your will be done in this mess. I can't, but You can, and if You want me to teach tonight, You'll have to tell me what to teach and then help me get to the meeting. I've had it!"

She continued to leaf through the Bible, and then her eyes were attracted to these words in Ephesians

86

4:29–32, and they seemed to all but leap from the page:

"Do not use harmful words in talking. Use only helpful words, the kind that build up and provide what is needed, so that you will do good to those who hear you; and do not make God's Holy Spirit sad; for the Spirit is God's mark of ownership on you, a guarantee that the day will come when God will set you free. Get rid of all bitterness, passion, and anger. No more shouting or insults! No more hateful feelings of any sort! Instead be kind and tender-hearted to one another, as God has forgiven you in Christ."

She had read that passage before but always in a good frame of mind. This time she had read it while bearing the anger and bitterness it spoke so emphatically against and this time the words cut deep. Her first reaction was, "O, Lord, I'm sorry, forgive me" and then her eyes fell on the cartoon at the top of the page and she began to laugh. The anger was gone, and she went back to the dishes. When I came back in the house she called me into the kitchen.

"Dearie," she laughed. "I just found a scripture

that fits you to a 'T' and even a picture to go with it. Look at that guy. He's your spittin' image!"

I read through it quickly and I couldn't help laughing either. It was all to appropriate to be denied. We went on laughing together. The written word of God had taken away the anger and replaced it with love. We later went on to the meeting. Joanne had insisted she still had nothing to offer in the way of instruction, but I insisted she did and I called upon her about halfway through the meeting, not to embarrass her but because I really did feel she would be able to offer something, however simple it might be. She swallowed hard and offered a quick prayer for guidance as she walked up to the microphone.

"I don't have any prepared instruction tonight," she said. "Instead I just want to share with you something that happened at home this afternoon. We learned a lot from it and I hope that now you'll be able to learn something from it, too." She then proceeded to give a blow-by-blow account of that afternoon's events at home, finishing by having them all turn to Ephesians 4 and look at the picture and then read the passage. They all laughed and, furthermore, they were laughing at me! I didn't mind, though, because I knew we all had much to gain from it. Joanne continued:

"In conclusion, I want to point out two very important things:

"First, as Christians, none of us can afford to harbor anger or bitterness in our hearts. The longer we keep it, the bigger it becomes until it eventually will get us into situations we never intended to be in. We are to be channels of God's Holy Spirit, and unless we daily repent of such sins as anger and bitterness, thereby putting them out of the way, then we're walking around with clogged channels.

"Second, I believe Christianity has to begin at home in our own families. If we continually get clogged there, then each time we leave to go out, we'll only be going out to clog the world.

"As you can readily see, life at the rectory is not one bit week-long Prayer and Praise meeting any more than it is at your house. How we all need to learn to be more effective Christians at home so we can be more effective Christians elsewhere in the world!

It was simple, humorous and they got the message. Joanne had spoken many times before but never had gotten the tremendous response she got that night as people so readily identified with our own personal struggle.

It isn't any easier for us than it is for you, but we, too, are attempting to become more of a Jesus family by learning to yield more and more to His Spirit in our lives.

10. NEVER, NEVER, NEVER

Although the major emphasis in this book is on the gift of the baptism in the Holy Spirit, please, my friends, *never, never, never* lost sight of the fact that the Gift of all Gifts is *salvation!* All other gifts are inferior. All other gifts are given to serve this foremost of gifts. All the miraculous gifts of the Spirit will end "when what is perfect comes," but the gift of salvation will never end. (I Corinthians 13:8–10)

Please understand that the power offered to us through the baptism in the Holy Spirit is power to spread the good news of salvation. Even before the day of Pentecost, when Jesus sent the 72 out to heal the sick, they became more involved with the power He had given them to heal and cast out demons than they did with the purpose of that power: to let people know that the Kingdom of God had come near them. We are told that when they returned with joy, saying "Even the demons obeyed us when we commanded them in your name," Jesus reproved them:

"Listen! I have given you authority, so that you can walk on snakes and scorpions, and over all the power of the Enemy, and nothing will hurt you. But don't be glad because the evil spirits obey you; rather be glad because your names are written in heaven." (Luke 10:17–20)

I have been holding regular weekly healing services at St. Martin's for the past 13 years. God has most definitely worked through those services, and many have been healed both spiritually and physically. However, it has only been in the past three years that we have come to see more frequent and tangible evidence of His healing power. Over these past three years, while there has obviously been much teaching on the baptism in the Holy Spirit, this teaching has always been heavily weighted with the primary need to accept Jesus as Lord and Saviour first. I emphasized salvation more than I had ever emphasized it before. Consequently, our people grew to better understand and appreciate this gift of all gifts. When they did, we began to see a very definite increase in the gifts of healing. Could it be that God wanted me to preach and teach His most precious gift of salvation first, lest it be overshadowed by premature involvement with His lesser gift of healing? I wonder.

As you read the following stories of healing, keep in mind that as miraculous as they are, they still are only secondary to the greater miracle of salvation. The gift of physical healing is but temporary in that we all will die some day. The gift of salvation is eternal.

Bill and Ruthmary shook hands with me as they were leaving the church on Sunday morning. Just three days earlier they had been in an automobile accident and Ruthmary had suffered a whiplash. When I inquired about her injury, Bill replied,

"I'm afraid she's no better. In fact, she's getting worse. She can't turn her head at all now. We have an appointment with the doctor tomorrow."

I suggested that they wait until I had finished greeting everyone so we could go back into the church for prayer. They agreed. We had a guest minister with us that day. He and I, along with Bill and Ruthmary and their two young sons, went up to the altar rail. When we finished praying, Bill began to speak to his wife.

"Ruthmary . . . ," he said, whereupon she immediately turned her head to look at him. It was obvious to all of us right then and there that she had been completely healed. The scene following was one of joyful tears and much thanksgiving (during which Bill quietly asked for and received the baptism in the Holy Spirit).

Nancy had been doctoring for psoriasis, an annoying skin condition, for four months. Her dermatologist was treating her with cortisone and tranquilizers and warned her that the disease could break out all over her body at one time even though she was on his prescribed medication. She resented the regular weekly visits to his office but was afraid of what might happen if she did not go. In addition, her medication was only prescribed to last one week, so it was necessary for her to see him each time in order to have the prescription refilled. Upon receiving salvation and this baptism in the Holy Spirit, she was given the faith to turn the entire situation over to the Lord. When she did, much of her related fear was dissolved and the psoriasis began to disappear. For six weeks she chose not to visit the doctor, but when she finally did, he was amazed at the change in her and her condition. He was further amazed once he looked at her record and saw she had not been on any medication for six weeks. That was well over a year ago. Nancy hasn't been back to the doctor since then. She is a typical example of what God can do when we let Him.

Ray had glaucoma for 14 years. Pressure from the resulting fluid in his eyes had reached so high from time to time that on three different occasions he was forced to quit the night school he was attending and finally had to give it up altogether. He had prayed for his eyes to be healed but, as he puts it, "I didn't really think it could happen to me." Almost two years ago in August, he received the baptism in the Holy Spirit and began to pray with more conviction, earnestly believing in God's healing power. The following November, he went for his regular quarterly checkup. After examining his eyes, the doctor spoke to him almost as if he wasn't quite sure what he was saying.

"Ray, I don't think you have glaucoma any more! But I don't want you to take my word for it. Stay off your medication for one week and then have my associate examine you."

That he did. One week later found Ray listening to the reassuring report of a second doctor:

"You don't need your eye drops any more. You don't have glaucoma!"

Ray has returned to night school, this time at a local Bible college. He's 'hitting the books' harder than ever and does some drafting work as well. His eyes offer him no problem whatsoever. God has healed them.

Two and a half year old Theresa lay in a local hospital, critically ill with cancer. Her doctors had given her only a few months to live. Nancy, who worked near Theresa's home as a volunteer, heard about her condition. She went home and told her husband, Fred, about her and they both went to visit Theresa one night. They could see the large lumps on both of her arms and legs as well as along her spine. She was crying in pain and the nurse let them hold her in their arms. Fred and Nancy have three young children of their own, but as they held her that night, they knew they were both "adopting" Theresa in their hearts. They prayed that she would be healed and especially that she would be relieved of her pain. The next morning, as one nurse later reported, "She woke up happy for the first time." That same night, Fred and Nancy came to our Prayer and Praise meeting and requested that we all pray for her recovery. That was Tuesday. By the following weekend, every lump had disappeared from the little girl's body. The doctors were amazed and again put her through every test they had given her previously. This time every test came back negative. They sent her home.

"It has to be a miracle," one doctor said, "we can't explain it any other way."

During one Tuesday night meeting a few months later, some of us were somewhat annoyed to hear a child squirming and jibbering during our prayer time. When it came time for Sharing, Fred and

Nancy introduced us to Theresa, who then proceeded to run up and down the middle aisle while we all stood and praised and thanked the Lord for His miracle of healing in her precious little body.

Ruth, our choir directress, came to our fall retreat with her right arm in a sling and a collar supporting her neck. She was suffering from chronic tendonitus of her right shoulder. In addition to the accompanying pain, she was further annoyed by not having the use of her right arm. She needed that arm in teaching school as well as in directing our choirs. The retreat did not end until breakfast on Sunday, but I had to leave early Saturday night. After I left, the group began to minister to one another in prayer, and some of them prayed that Ruth would be healed. As they did, she experienced a sudden cessation of pain and discovered that she was able to raise her arm. The next morning after rehearsing the junior and senior choirs before the service, she made the usual announcements and then a special one.

"I have one more announcement to make," she said joyfully. "I had prayer for my tendonitus at the retreat last night. Since then I have had no medication nor have I had any pain. I've been healed. Praise the Lord!"

One week later, about 20 minutes before our Sunday morning service, I asked Ruth if she would consent to being a "live" sermon illustration. She agreed and, at the appropriate time in my sermon, she stepped into the pulpit and shared the details of her healing with the entire congregation.

Probably the most commonly asked question concerning Christian healing is, "Why are some healed and others not?" I don't think anyone can answer that question, and I would not care to meet an individual who thought he could. Of course we know that "God's ways are not our ways." Sometimes in His mysterious ways, the spirit is healed and the body is not. Such was the case with Sydney.

Sydney and his wife, Olive, came to St. Martin's in 1964. Both were natives of England and Sydney had served on the staff of the British Embassy in Washington before assuming a position as division manager with a research company in Monroeville. He and his wife were quickly accepted by the people of St. Martin's. The following year found him president of the Men's Club and not long after that, he was elected to the vestry. He rarely missed a Sunday morning service. Almost every Sunday I could look back and see Sydney and Olive seven pews from the front of the left side by the aisle. He often made a point of commenting on, or questioning, something I had said in my sermon.

Then that fearful day arrived. Sydney had been sent to the hospital for tests and was told he had cancer. The bottom fell out of his life. From that time on, he was on and off his job and in and out of the hospital. With his scientific mind, he began to read medical journals and, by knowing the various changes in the medication the doctors gave him, he was able to determine each consecutive stage of his illness as he reached it.

In the last few months of his life, he grasped at anything to find peace and reassurance, but nothing seemed to satisfy. He could not bear to be alone. This was especially difficult for Olive, so the men of our Brotherhood of St. Andrew set up a schedule whereby two men visited him every evening. As often as possible, I would get there as they were leaving to be with him later in the evening. One night Sydney and I talked at great length and he reveiewed his entire life for me. Before I left, he confessed his sins and I pronounced the Absolution.

A few weeks later, on the day he died, Olive and I stood by his bedside. He had lapsed into a coma. I offered prayer for him and shortly after a few sounds began to come from his lips. It sounded much like one of our hymns, but I said nothing to Olive because I wasn't really sure. After he died, Olive and I walked down the corridor together and, despite her extreme grief, she spoke.

"You know, Mr. Stockhowe, I think Sydney was singing a hymn in those last few minutes just before he died."

"You know, Olive, I had exactly the same reaction."

Who could possibly explain why Sydney was not healed physically? I can't begin to even try, but I have no doubt in my own mind that before he died he had come to know Jesus better than he'd ever known Him before.

These are only a few of the more dramatic in stances of healing we have either seen or heard of. Much more numerous are the healings that seldom make headlines but are just as edifying and beautiful to those involved in them: a child's earache, a football player's injured knee, a mother's allergy, another's thyroid, yet another's stomach ulcer, a kidney infection or just the flu or a common cold—all of these and more healed through the power of prayers, most of them prayed at home by the loved-ones involved.

I don't ignore those in the medical profession, however. I know God definitely works through them when He so chooses. My advice has always been and will continue to be: pray first, then phone the doctor. Luke is referred to by Paul as the "beloved physician." There's nothing in his gospel that indicates Luke ever had to give up his medical profession in order to serve the Lord. I thank God for the availability and talents of our doctors, dentists, nurses and technicians. They are all instruments of His healing power, but I also thank God for the times He chooses to work without those instruments in order to further remind us of His supreme power.

11. WHAT DIFFERENCE DOES IT MAKE?

"So many of your congregation *do* claim that they have received the baptism in the Holy Spirit and they *do* claim to know Jesus better than ever before—so what? What difference does it make? What difference does it make in their lives? What difference has it made in your church?"

I am often confronted with these and similar questions, and I assume that by now you are wondering much the same thing. What better way to show some of the many differences than to let members of our congregation speak for themselves. Some of their stories are dramatic, some are not so dramatic, but each of them reveal various differences in their lives since they have come to know that "Jesus is alive!"

*　　*　　*

Marcia's story wouldn't be here if it weren't for the Christian love and concern of two of her friends who had already come to know that Jesus is alive.

In late February of 1969 I asked Jesus to come into my heart and life, and on March 28 of the same year I received the baptism in the Holy Spirit. So ended almost 42 years of a personal wilderness, and began the birth of a "new creation in Christ Jesus." I'm not proud of the person I was before I met the Lord, but I'm grateful for the experiences because they make this new life just that much more precious.

As part of their Lenten program, one of the local churches had invited Muriel to give her School of Prayer. Two very loving and concerned friends talked me into going. I'm sure if I'd known at the time that they were praying for God to touch me, I'd have been highly indignant. Religion was a very private thing to me, and while I had a nominal belief in God, I seldom called on Him for help (and wasn't about to have anyone do it for me). I went, rather belligerently, and God really began to move. Muriel had a peace and joy radiating from her which I couldn't identify, but which I knew immediately I wanted. Furthermore, with almost embarrassing frankness, she talked about God as if she knew Him, and yet she didn't strike me as some sort of religious nut. She introduced me to Jesus, and told me He loved me, and with those few words, my life changed.

The first time I entered the red doors of St. Martin's church, I was intoxicated ... not with the fullness of the Holy Spirit, but with the fullness of 90-proof bourbon! In those days I was rapidly becoming more and more dependent on alcohol and tranquilizers to help me face a life I was trying to escape. I was an alcoholic, and my nerves had reached such a state that most of the time my whole body shook unless I was sedated in some way. God, in His great mercy, kept me from seeing myself as I was then, nor did I realize that the personal hell I was going through was felt by my family and friends. It's not important to go into any more details of my background, except to say that my encounter with Christ came at a time when I was about as low spiritually, emotionally and physically as a soul can get. I was seriously considering suicide because I hated my life and what I'd become.

But someone told me Jesus loved me, and when I first started going to St. Martin's I heard it again. In all my life, no one had ever told me this before. I didn't know He even knew me. Once again I saw this joy and peace on people's faces. I truly felt the love of Jesus in their presence, and I began to seek that love. I was full of questions. The world of spiritualism and the occult had been fascinating to me, and I'd invaded this dangerous territory, so I had a lot to "un-learn" and ask forgiveness for. This whole business of being "born again" (salvation) was foreign to me. I'd never heard it preached, and it seemed incredible that forgiveness and a new chance were mine just for the asking. I thank God for the patience He gave those wonderful people in ministering to me. They and many others were of tremendous help to this new Christian baby.

What's happened since March of 1969 is pretty spectacular to me. I was instantly delivered of the need or desire for drugs ... I've given up alcohol and a three-pack-a-day cigarette habit. I'm a happy woman. I'm a better wife and mother, and I have that wonderful inner peace that truly passes understanding. I don't know God's plan for me for the future, but I know that He has one, and most of all, I know He does love me.

*   *   *

Paul and his wife, Jacquie, both in their early 30s, have been members of St. Martin's for six years now. Paul is on our vestry and Jacquie is our Director of Religious Education.

HIS

What changes have taken place in my life since my turning to Jesus as Lord and Saviour? I'm sure each person who has made this commitment could answer this question differently. Our Lord has a habit of starting His development of you wherever you are. In a word, I think freedom would best describe this new life in Christ for me. "Freedom from what?" you might rightly ask. Well, freedom to love other people for one. I wasn't even able to love myself until Jesus showed me His grace made me worthy of His love. Then He let me see that others had many of the same doubts and fears I had. When I "saw" this, not with my eyes, but with my heart, I began reaching outward instead of withdrawing. Another is freedom from the fears of insecurity and death. As the apostle Paul writes, "If God is for us who can be against us?" Once I put Jesus first I became free of the rush and turmoil of acquiring material things. And the most amazing thing happened—I found that I enjoyed the things we have far more than ever before. Since being baptized by Jesus with the Holy Spirit, another new and completely unexpected freedom has developed: that is the freedom through God's power (not mine) to talk to others about Him. Recently Jacquie and I spent a Faith Alive weekend in Rochester, New York. A Faith Alive weekend is a form of lay witness mission. Lay people are invited by a church or group of churches to come and share just what Jesus means to them in their lives. At this weekend in Rochester the Lord had me lead a small discussion group one night and give a public witness another night. Three years ago I wouldn't have attended such a mission even as an observer had one been held right in our own church.

How has this freedom come about? Trust, I think, is the key. For by trusting in Him, He cam provide for all our needs. Trusting requires yielding, completely yielding as much of myself as I can muster. It isn't always easy but I know now it's the only way. These have truly been the three most joyous years of my life. Praise God!

HERS

Jesus has changed my own life in two major ways. One way is in dealing with my daily life. Since He baptized me in His Holy Spirit He has been helping me root out hangups, understand them and give them to Him. This frees me, and as I grow to be more and more open to the Holy Spirit's teaching and guidance, I am becoming more aware of the needs of those involved in my daily life. Now that my eyes are on Jesus more and less on myself—or *my* needs, *my* desires, *my* fears—I can better love and understand my husband, children, family, friends, neighbors, and the children I teach. Before being baptized in the Holy Spirit I never really stopped to think about the deep inner feelings of others. Now I am beginning to, and because of Jesus' love I can treat them with love.

The other way Jesus has changed my life is in crisis situations. Three months ago my mother, only 53 years old, died after battling cancer for a year. I don't have just some vague hope that this is not the end of her life. I have a very certain knowledge that her spirit is with Jesus and that I will see her again in the next life. I don't know why she had to die now or with cancer, but I do know, because of the love of God I have felt in my own life, that God loves my mother very much too. I know he had a good reason for permitting her to die, even though I can't understand it. The Holy Spirit has abundantly given of his comfort and strength so that I can bear our temporary separation.

OURS

Our life together and our relationship with our two little girls has felt the healing touch of Jesus Christ. He has healed emotional problems, binding our wounds in love, so that bitterness, loneliness, anger, resentment—all the things that make sore spots and walls come between loved ones—can be given to Him and not buried inside us. We are able not only to pray for one another but to pray for small things and big things alike, whether it be for help in picking out just the right birthday puppy, for help with sadness or anger, for guidance in choosing the job and the house our heavenly Father knows is right for us, or for physical healing through the power of Jesus Christ, our great physician and healer. One of our greatest joys has been to hear the praise of Jesus on the lips of our children and to see them turn to him so freely with simple prayers.

"Mommy, I asked Jesus to help me in kindergarten today."

"Dear Jesus, help Mommy not be mad."

"Dear God, I like you. Amen."

*　　*　　*

Bob and Marilyn are in their 30s. Bob is on our vestry and Marilyn teaches Sunday School. Marilyn writes:

Our whole family has changed in these past two years. Our three young children have also become aware that Jesus is alive and is in their presence always. We are no longer just a happy family trying to do things on our own, but a closely knit family coming together to God our heavenly Father with all our concerns. We know that because of the life and death of our Lord Jesus Christ, we do not have to struggle through life on our own, carrying all our burdens with us. All too many times we falter, but Jesus in His great mercy forgives us and picks us up right where we are.

It is not unusual for any of our children to come to us and say, "I don't feel well. Will you pray with me and ask Jesus to make me better?" Jesus has instantly healed earaches in the middle of the night. He has healed upset stomachs and taken the fire out of burned fingers, along with many other miracles. Last spring as I was painting, He helped me spread a scant one quarter of a gallon of paint so that it covered the walls of both our dining room and our hallway. When I finished and thought, "This is impossible!" His answer was:

"Didn't I feed 5,000 with five loaves and two fishes?"

One rainy evening last November, we were traveling to Massachusetts to spend the Thanksgiving holiday with our families, when a car traveling in the wrong direction on a divided highway nearly caused a head-on collision. As our car swerved to avoid hitting the other car, we went into a skid. My husband and I, along with our two oldest children, ages ten and seven, began praying out loud, asking God in the name of Jesus to protect us. Our car stopped in the middle of the medial strip, heading in the wrong direction, but no one was hurt and except for the loss of two hubcaps, no damage was done to our car. We thanked God for our safety. We found out what it means to trust God in all situations.

We have had our times of sorrow and disappointment as well as times of joy; but when we let the Lord guide and direct us, there is always a new and greater understanding of the love God has for us.

We praise and thank God for the many blessings He has so freely showered upon our lives and pray that we may be more open to His great love and compassion. We look forwrd to the time when we will be united with Him and His heavenly kingdom.

* * *

Angie and Gill have been members of St. Martin's for 14 years. They both sing in the choir and Bill is a past vestryman.

If someone would have said to me a few short years ago, "Jesus loves you," I would have accepted it but not really known the depths of that statement. Today, I know the reality of those words. Because of His love for me, I can love and care for others with the very fiber of my being.

Bill and I, along with our daughter, Jenan, were an ordinary suburban family with the usual trials and joys of most people in our area. We were interested in other people only in so far as they affected our own lives. Bill and I as a couple were engrossed with the social partying and bridging, and Jenan with her teenage activities. I ran the gamut of being active in many community organizations with special emphasis on Women's Club and duplicate bridge. It was exciting. In Women's Club I was in charge of a big money-making event, which gave me the prestige and recognition that were very important to me. I played bridge in countless tournaments with some small success. All three of us were active in church. I held office in the women's group and Bill was on the vestry. We were loyal church participants, but we didn't really know Jesus.

Another great passion of my life was my passion for clothes. I shopped, planned and shopped some more. Jenan and I both were the proverbial clothes-horses. However, even with the pride in what I had accomplished, I was beginning to feel the need for more meaning to my life. I went back to school to complete a degree in education which had been interrupted by my marriage. Going back to school was the path leading to my deep concern for young people. My motive for returning to school was purely selfish. We had a couple of experiences which made us feel the need of financial security. I know now that Bill and I had experienced God's mercy in so many ways even when we weren't aware of how much he cared. He saw us through the loss of Bill's finger in a company accident, through five months of caring for mother, her death, the shock of Bill being without a job, our son being in the service, and my constant fears, nerves and worrying.

About three years ago, Jean, one of my bridge buddies, began to give up some of her bridge playing to attend prayer meetings. I couldn't believe it! She was as much addicted to bridge as I, and yet she preferred to give up a bridge game just to go to a prayer group. I became almost belligerant about this situation. However, she was so content that I knew there must be something to her changed attitude. Through a series of complicated events and much skepticism I attended a meeting in Oakland to hear Nicky Cruz, a transformed gang leader from New York. The Lord touched me, I accepted Jesus as my Saviour and He baptized me with His Holy Spirit most dramatically. Jean was present and I knew beyond a shadow of a doubt that she had been praying for me. Today, we are prayer partners and share prayers, intercede and minister together. My family followed with similar experiences shortly after my conversion. Now Bill is active in the youth workshop at church and Jenan assists in the Sunday School.

More and more I seemed to be drawn to young people, mostly college youngsters. One evening, Jean's young college daughter, Dee, along with Jenan and some of their friends, were saying how much they would like to get together to discuss and learn more about the Bible and to share their problems. The Lord spoke to my heart, and I immediately suggested that Jean and I have a meeting at my home Friday night. Since then, college youngsters have been coming here every Friday night for fellowship, prayer and study. We never know who will be coming, but the Lord knows who has needs and sends them to us. Young men and women have accepted Jesus, received the baptism in the Holy Spirit and have been healed mentally, physically and spiritually.

Each meeting is different. One night we were praying for the Lord to heal Phyllis' back. We emphasized how much Jesus loved these youngsters and that he wanted them whole and Phyllis was healed.

We also explained to them about salvation and the baptism in the Holy Spirit, and Lydia asked us to pray with her. As we started to pray for Lydia, her friend Greg became extremely upset and fearful and left the room. He was really having a battle. We could see the struggle going on. His face and body showed evidence of a tremendous conflict. We kept praying for Lydia, but Jean and I were also praying silently for Greg. Finally, the battle was won and he came back into the room. He told us he had come to the meeting out of curiosity. All his friends were experimenting with sex and drugs and he didn't think Dee and George were for real. The meeting had shaken him up in more ways than one. Here was a group of his peers who looked like the average kids of today—long hair, jeans, bare feet—but who obviously had something "the average kid" didn't. They had an inner peace and joy and a strength that he wanted. Greg then asked us for prayer and he and Lydia both accepted Jesus and were baptized in His Holy Spirit. Jesus Christ was the overcomer.

Dave was another convert who was very much burdened. We watched the Lord take over as we prayed for Dave. He began to glow with the love of Jesus and tears of joy ran down his face. Husky, rugged Dave had no embarrassment but just excitement and utter amazement that the Lord cared for him.

There is Tom who said he couldn't accept the teaching of his church and then he met Jesus. Now he goes on many youth faith missions witnessing what the Lord has meant to him. He says now he can be high on Jesus and doesn't need to be high on pot.

My story of our Friday nights would not be complete, or even started, had it not been for Dee and George. They have been dating since high school and are our foundation stones. They are Christians who are living examples of what they believe. Most of the boys who have come are friends of George. He knows when they are spiritually hungry and he leads them to attend a meeting. We provide the place; Jean and I are there, but the Holy Spirit leads the meeting. Jenan attends and gives great joy with her guitar and singing, her ministry which is a gift from the Lord. We have to keep praying for some of our stray lambs like Chris and Timmy, who find it difficult to remain on the right path, but we praise God that they do come back.

These are but a few of the stories of the young people who are searching for meaning in their lives. We realize they still have problems but now they know they can come to their friends in Christ and ask for prayer and guidance. Most of all they know Jesus is the answer!

*   *   *

Jean, another choir member, is Angie's bridge buddy who eventually gave up her bridge meetings for prayer meetings.

Since finding salvation and then being baptized in the Holy Spirit, what seems important to me now is not to linger in these glorious doorways but to go on learning to live in this new dimension with the Holy Spirit as my guide and companion and trying to be obedient to His direction. Now that I've been on this joyous walk for three years I could write a volume about all the miracles of God's love which I've seen, but one night stands out in my memory.

It was Tuesday, and we were in the library for our weekly Prayer and Praise service. We were part way

111

through our singing when some of the Greeks began to arrive—not all at once but in groups and at intervals. What a handsome and happy group of people, brown eyes sparkling and white teeth flashing as they smiled and laughed in their enthusiastic greetings. And yet, for some unknown reason, I was entertaining critical thoughts about the appearance of some of the men. Their hair was too long, and their outfits too colorful and flamboyant to suite my somber mood. Actually, though, they were right in the style which is now acceptable for men of high fashion.

At the end of the service one of these young men, Art, was standing in the lobby of the church and trembling.

"I can't stop shaking," he said.

"You need the great physician," said our guitarist, Norman, taking his arm. "Come on, Jean. Let's pray for him."

Reluctantly I followed them into the sanctuary where Bill and Chuck joined us to help pray. Many of the Greek women were already there, and we prayed for all of them—some for salvation and some for the baptism in the Holy Spirit. A few received their new language of praise, and there was a babble of excited whisperings, prayers and tongues all mingled with tears and smiles. Then all at once I was filled with a mighty outpouring of the love of Jesus for everyone there, but most especially for John and Art, and I could only think:

"These are my brothers, and kneeling at this altar we are all one! How beautiful they are, their hair, their clothes, and especially their countenances!"

112

I suddenly realized that in His tender mercy, Jesus was allowing me to experience in a new way the boundless love He has for each one of us, His children. The next morning I was still filled with love, joy and excitement to such a degree that I was unable to read my Bible but could only weep before the Lord and praise and thank Him for His grace to me a sinner—me with all my pride and my ugly thoughts of criticism, especially for anything as unimportant as outward appearance.

This special sense of joy and love has never left me and has served to even further remind me that Jesus is alive!

*　　*　　*

George is one of the foundation stones Angie referred to. He is presently finishing his freshman year at Duquesne University.

I am studying for my degree in music. At the beginning of the school year the Lord brought me together with a friend named Doug. Some of the kids told me to stay away from him because he was "far out." My intention was not to be a good friend to him but to get some helpful hints from him on my musical instruments since he played the same instruments and had much more experience. At first it was very fascinating to hear Doug talk about his philosophy of life and how man is "nowhere" and the government is "nowhere." After awhile I realized why the Lord had brought us together. Doug was looking for all of the answers from within himself. He

113

had searched from Yoga to pot but still could not satisfy his own inner desires.

One day I was led to talk to Doug about Jesus. It didn't go over too well because Doug thought it was absurd to depend on a God that was alive some two thousand years ago. He thought Jesus was a man who prophesied good things about love. About two weeks went by and I kept praying that some of the talking would sink into Doug's head. The thing that impressed Doug the most was that God gives eternal life. He had heard it all before, but really never thought about it. When it came down to the point of dying or not dying, Doug started to think. He just couldn't figure out why I wasn't afraid to die.

We got into the Second Coming in another one of our discussions, and by this time Doug was believing that Jesus was the Son of God but not sure if he wanted to accept Him. I was led again to tell Doug about how Christ is going to come in a cloud and physically take the Christians up to heaven. Doug questioned me.

"What about the rest of the people?"

"I think they will be going to hell, Doug."

"I don't believe in hell," he said sarcastically.

"You'd better," I replied, "because that's where you are going to go if you don't accept Jesus."

That kind of ended the conversation for that night but I think it worked. I believe Doug started reading the Bible the next day. He was still confused after our last discussion. So I asked him to come out to talk to Mrs. C and Mrs. Z because they would be able to add to some of the things we talked about.

After Doug saw the love in the two women's faces, he couldn't resist the love Jesus was offering him. We all prayed for him, Doug asked the Lord to give him salvation and he also was baptized in the Holy Spirit. Within a month's time Doug's brother and ten other young kids accepted Jesus and received the baptism in the Holy Spirit. Witnessing about Jesus to others had always raised me to a new spiritual level, but this experience with Doug really brought me closer to Him than ever.

Since I have accepted Jesus, I get along so much better with my parents. I can honestly say I love my mother and father 100% more than I used to. I can get along with my mother's nagging. (She really doesn't nag, but that's what I call it.) I learned to understand, rather than just cope with, my father's moods. We still have our problems as a family, but somehow with Jesus it's a lot easier for me to say I'm sorry.

* * *

Faye is another of our college students who has taken the Good News to her college campus.

I've been a member of St. Martin's for about 16 years and have always loved it and served it with joy. I sang in two or three different choirs, attended Sunday School regularly and served as an officer in the youth fellowship. But on August 30, 1968, I came into the experience of knowing Jesus personally and not just knowing *about* Him. I attended a Billy Graham Crusade in Pittsburgh and went forward to give my life to Him. That was the real turning point in

115

my life. I went back to St. Martin's and continued doing all the things I'd done before in the church—only now with new devotion and zeal because I was serving my Lord and Saviour. I began to have an unquenchable thirst for the Scriptures and an overpowering desire to be closer to Jesus in every way. This desire led me to the baptism in the Holy Spirit, which has given me the courage and boldness to share my experience with others.

That brings me to where I am today—a sophomore at Marietta College in Ohio. This is where I've been able to put all my experience to the test. Peer pressures are strong, drugs are the norms rather than the exception, people are experimenting with all sorts of devices, experiences, and drugs that will help them to "put it together"—help them understand themselves and know where they're going and why. Satan inhabits this world and in no place is this fact more demonstrated than on the college campus. But my generation can detect a phony, they can see a "cop-out" a mile away. That's why my experience with Jesus has to be something that can be lived day by day and which never fails.

Wherever the disciples went in the New Testament, a church, defined as a body of believers, was established. In the same way God has provided a church at Marietta. Marietta, a non-affiliated college with no Christian fellowship to speak of at the beginning of this year, now has a functioning body of Christ of perhaps 20 to 25 college students. My brothers and sisters here come from various backgrounds, have various interests and plans, but have a common motivation—that of glorifying the name of

Jesus with every facet of their lives. Each person's personal experience with Jesus has given him the boldness to be a witness and tell of the changing power of the resurrected Jesus Christ in any hungry heart. As more and more people on this campus come to know Him, we become more and more aware of His steadfastness. We see the need of depending on Him for all things, material and spiritual.

Trusting the Lord Jesus with your entire life truly does lead to a peace that passes understanding.

* * *

June and her husband Lloyd are "almost" charter members of St. Martin's. They've been there almost as long as I have. It seems appropriate, then, to end my story of our people "up here on the hill" by letting June tell what she sees as she looks back over all her years with us.

Our family has belonged to St. Martin's almost 15 years now ... almost since the first service was held in the old neighborhood social hall. Nostalgia flows when we "old timers" reminisce. ...

"Remember nailing board to board Saturday after Saturday until we finally finished that church school building?"

"Remember serving lentil soup and ham sandwiches to our husbands that blustery morning they put up the roof?"

"Remember hunting that obscure wholesale ribbon store in New York City just to cut a few pennies overhead from a bazaar item?"

117

We worked hard for the Lord in those days too and our "common causes" bound us in endearing friendships that we will never forget. Our labors should have left us feeling very rewarded.

But often they did not. I remember scolding Father Stockhowe because I thought he put too little pressure on the men of our congregation to help the faithful few who regularly plugged away at the church school addition. Another time I told him, "You know, I neglect so many other duties to do church work, I'm beginning to feel guilty about being in church!" In those days I dragged our tiny daughters from church "coffee," to meeting, to workshop, then scolded them when they interrupted my church-centered phone calls. Helping the Lord wasn't easy, especially when the best I seemed able to earn for Him, at considerable cost to myself, was about 50 cents an hour!

More serious than such material frustrations, however, was the inadequate way we tried to help fellow parishioners in distress. We had our share of troubles, including suicides, breakdowns and infant deaths. Each event shook us severely because, as a congregation, we were exceptionally close. We *did* ask God's help. We rallied like a swarm of bees when a member experienced hard times. We held weekly healing services. We memorialized with Easter lilies and hymnals and candlesticks. Wanting to do all I could, I joined these rather formal acts with desperate fervor and impoverished expectations.

How different things are now! I remember one Wednesday morning in the "good old days." Our study group had been boldly arguing the "possibilities" of Christianity when one of our members became ill. Since I'm a nurse, Father Stockhowe asked me to stay with her while he made emergency medical arrangements. There she sat, frozen in so rigid a pose that only her tears moved. While she slipped into an acute depression I helplessly patted her arm and told her everything would be all right.

Incredible! I never even prayed silently, "Help us, Lord." I reassured her that her doctor would help her, but I didn't know Jesus well enough to recommend Him! Oh, I guess with some awkwardness I could have said, "We'll pray for you," meaning, "We'll submit an application for your well-being to this God, whom I hear sometimes does remarkable things for worthwhile people." But never, as now, would I have urged, "Please, get in touch with my *physician*, Jesus Christ. He's already promised to help you and is waiting for your call." Never, as now, would I have been led to ask, "May I pray with you?"

The *good old* days? They can't compare with these *GOOD NEWS* days—these days since we've experienced what I think of as the Great Breakthrough, with the baptism in the Holy Spirit. For me, the great breakthrough came the moment I finally leveled with God . . . the moment I was able to say at last, "I'm sick of hedging, God . . . and I know that You know I am a fake." At that moment, He told me He was real . . . real enough to talk to . . . real enough to trust with big problems and little details . . . real enough to recommend.

And what a privilege to recommend Him. A few

weeks ago a young man who recognized that he was having a remission of a depression, which had taken him several years of hospitalization to conquer, came to our Prayer and Praise meeting and openly asked for help. We prayed, and God healed him. We were overjoyed, but not surprised. Again and again God has shown us this kind of reality:

- evenings of fellowship much too brief for all who would like to share stories of how Jesus is alive in their everyday worlds
- hours of enthusiastic labor upon which no price can be set
- moments of prayerful waiting for direction from God.

We share a whole new way of life now. Sure, we still have the bazaars and the do-it-yourself work sessions. But just listen to the change in the conversations going on as paint-spattered parishioners brush trim to the woodwork. They are talking about the before-school prayer group their youngsters started; about the anonymous $50 contribution St. Martin's received with the attached note, "Please keep that roof-top sign, JESUS IS ALIVE, lit"; about the family's experience delivering Christmas toys and food to a needy family. Impromptu strains of "Praise the Lord" echo through the parish hall, while in the hush of the chancel, several men kneel in prayer.

How does one feel, belonging to a congregation whom God has so blessed? I can tell you. Very loved. And very fortunate.

It's thrilling to be a small part of God's great outpouring, and, quite frankly, it's exciting to belong to a parish which has prestige (and some notoriety) because of it's spiritual activity. I cannot help feeling gratified when I see the many spiritually hungry people who come from miles away to be fed at St. Martin's. The messages brought to St. Martin's by simple laymen and internationally prominent leaders alike have literally changed my life . . . and the lives of my entire family.

And the change goes a lot deeper than the mere joy of being a parishioner of St. Martin's. Six years ago we moved to a neighboring community but continued to attend St. Martin's. Now our new community is starting an Episcopal mission, and our friends and neighbors have asked us to help. Can you see our dilemma—to want to serve Jesus as a responsible Christian neighbor, and yet, to be asked to leave our beloved St. Martin's to do so?

"Dear God, what shall we do?" we asked.

While we waited for direction, we continued to fulfill our church school and choir commitments at St. Martin's.

In the meantime, a job opportunity, one which my husband would probably not have investigated in the *good old* days, came up. We prayed about this, too, and God has taken care of all details, even to the point of selling our house. We'd made no arrangements to show the house during church hours. But while we were at church a friend had borrowed a table from us and inadvertently left the sliding glass door unlocked. House-hunters looking through the door noticed it was unlocked, and asked neighbors to show them the house. Minutes later, they bought it.

So we are leaving St. Martin but with a feeling of tremendous peace and expectation. One parishioner said, when we told him we were leaving:

"How wonderful! I know God has something great waiting for you there!"

His joyful remark reflects the security and freedom offered the believer who knows "Jesus is alive!"

12. IT'S ONLY THE BEGINNING

The baptism in the Holy Spirit is not an end in itself. It is not a shortcut. It is only the beginning. It merely opens the way to a greater realization that Jesus is alive. We then have to press on toward that ultimate goal God has placed before us, His goal for us to be conformed to the image of His Son, Jesus Christ. Pressing on toward that goal is demanding. There is no easy way through. If a believer, upon receiving the baptism, does not press on, then its intended blessings are lost and he becomes a stumbling block to others as well as himself.

Once received, the power of the Holy Spirit cannot be saved and carried around in a box to be used at our own leisure. It must be applied daily to every area of our lives. That's what St. Paul meant when he spoke of walking in the Spirit. Walking in the Spirit is not some spooky, mystical, high in-the-clouds experience. It means simply on-the-spot yielding to the power of God's Holy Spirit in every situation that comes along. It is letting the Holy Spirit do what we cannot do for ourselves. To walk in the Spirit is to meet every situation of life, regardless of how simple or difficult it may be with the prayer, "Lord, I can't, but You can." We can be conformed to the perfect image of Jesus Christ only to the degree that we walk in the Spirit. We can never be conformed while walking after the flesh. As Paul put it:

"How can you be so foolish! You began by God's Spirit; do you now want to finish by your own power?" (Galatians 3:3)

The highway to perfection is a narrow and difficult one. Accepting salvation gives us the privilege to travel that highway. The baptism in the Holy Spirit then gives us an abundance of power for the long trip that lies ahead:

"And a highway shall be there, and it shall be called the Holy Way; the unclean shall not pass over it, and the fools shall not err therein." (Isaiah 35:8 RSV)

The one main condition for moving along on this highway of holiness is obedience. To obey the word of God is to go forward. To disobey is to go off into the ditch that lies on both sides. In Acts 2:41–42 RSV, Luke gives us four disciplines necessary in order to continue down that highway in obedience and avoid the ditches:

"So those who received his word were baptized, and there were added that day about three thousand souls. And they devoted themselves to the apostles' teaching and fellowship, to the breaking of bread and the prayers."

I like to think of these four disciplines as the wheels on a car: teaching, fellowship, breaking of bread, and prayer. A Christian cannot continue steadfastly down the highway of holiness when any one of these wheels is missing or out of balance. Missing wheels only get us off the highway and into a ditch. Almost without exception, when I see a believer wavering in his faith, I can also see neglect on his part in one or more of these four areas. There is no substitute for any one of them. The three thousand needed them all then. We need them all today.

Teaching. To those three thousand souls after Pentecost, the apostles' teaching had to be taught by word of mouth. We, today, have that same teaching recorded in our Bibles. All of us need to turn daily to both the Old and New Testaments for our personal guidance and inspiration. Hosea 4:6 reads, "My people are destroyed for lack of knowledge," referring to the deliberate ignorance of the Israelites. We, too, can be destroyed spiritually by our deliberate neglect to learn and understand what God is saying to us through His written Word. As Christians, we have accepted Jesus Christ as our Lord and Saviour. Through Him we have been given our inheritance in the Kingdom of God. Along with that inheritance God has given us an "owner's manual," the Holy Bible—that we might better know and understand all that we've inherited and better use it to His glory. To neglect our "owner's manual" is to neglect our inheritance.

Fellowship. This, too, is necessary to good Christian living. There is much strength to be found in rubbing elbows with others who are moving down the same highway as we. Regular church attendance is imperative, but Sunday morning does not provide adequate time for sharing our personal interests and concern with one another. We all need and should seek the informal type fellowship to be found through phone conversations or an occasional afternoon or evening with other believers in their homes. While some Prayer and Praise meetings can provide this kind of fellowship, they often grow in attendance until much of the opportunity for that needed personal touch becomes lost. Make a habit of getting together often with those who share you love for our Lord. It's essential to our spiritual well-being and you'll love every minute of it. In the words of that old familiar hymn:

"Blest be the tie that binds our hearts in Christian love.
The fellowship of kindred minds is like to that above."

Breaking of Bread. I believe this refers to Holy Communion. Just as Jesus commanded His disciples to go preach, teach, and baptize in His name, so He also commanded them at the Last Supper to do this in remembrance of me." He instituted this sacrament as a means of grace (in the words of our Episcopalian service) that we may have "the innumerable benefits procured unto us by the same." To neglect Holy Communion is to disobey our Lord's command and ignore one of the means of grace He has made available to us.

Prayer. Last, but obviously not least, is prayer. It is interesting to realize that the disciples directly asked Jesus to teach them only one thing, "Lord teach us to pray." (Luke 11:1) They knew Jesus always gave first priority to prayer and we have to learn to do the same. How often should we pray? Paul tells us in I Thessalonians 5:17 to "pray at all times." No matter where you are in your personal prayer life, don't be satisfied. There's more.

It takes good old-fashioned discipline to stay on the highway to holiness. There is no other way.

"Do not deceive yourselves: no one makes a fool of God. A man will reap exactly what he plants." (Galatians 6:7)

SUGGESTED READING

They Speak with Other Tongues, John Sherril

If I Can You Can, Betty Lee Esses*

It Can Happen to Anybody!, Russell Bixler*

A Scriptural Outline of the Baptism in the Holy Spirit, George and Harriet Gillies*

Power for the Body of Christ, Rev. Michael Harper

As at the Beginning, Rev. Michael Harper

Ministering the Baptism in the Holy Spirit, Don Basham*

Speaking in Tongues, a Gift for the Body of Christ, Rev. Larry Christenson*

The Christian Family, Rev. Larry Christenson*

A Handbook on Holy Spirit Baptism, Rev. Don Basham*

Receiving the Holy Spirit, Rev. Robert Hall

Face Up with a Miracle, Rev. Don Basham*

Nine O'Clock in the Morning, Rev. Dennis Bennett

Please Make Me Cry, Cookie Rodriguez*

A Handbook on Tongues, Interpretation and Prophecy, Rev. Don Basham*

The Holy Spirit and You, Rev. Dennis Bennett

Catholic Pentecostals, Kevin and Dorothy Ranaghan

* Available from Whitaker House.

PAPERBACK BOOKS PUBLISHED
BY WHITAKER
WHEREVER PAPERBACKS ARE SOLD
OR USE ORDER FORM